Pound's Cantos Declassified

POUND'S CANTOS DECLASSIFIED

Philip Furia

———————

THE PENNSYLVANIA STATE UNIVERSITY PRESS
UNIVERSITY PARK AND LONDON

Library of Congress Cataloging in Publication Data

Furia, Philip, 1943-
Pound's Cantos declassified.

Includes index.
1. Pound, Ezra, 1885-1972. Cantos. I. Title.
PS3531. 82C2853   1984   811'.52   83-43227
ISBN 0-271-00373-1

For Karen

Contents

Preface

I hope this book will be helpful to readers who already know *The Cantos* as well as to those approaching Pound's epic for the first time. Unlike most other studies of *The Cantos*, which treat the poem's beautiful lyrical passages, *Pound's Cantos Declassified* concentrates on those vast stretches composed, not of Pound's own poetry, nor of poetry at all in the usual sense, but of that most unpoetic of forms, the document. For Pound, such documents contain the "luminous details" of history that "give one a sudden insight" into "the intelligence of a period." Although they are "hard to find," such luminous details are "swift and easy of transmission" and "govern knowledge as the switchboard governs an electric circuit."[1] I have tried to show how Pound brought out of these documents both their poetic power and their historical significance, but I always remind myself, and encourage the new reader of Pound to recognize, that *The Cantos* are first and foremost a poem. If I refrain from adding my own observations on the lyrical brilliance of that poem, it is only because it has been so aptly illuminated by other critics.

For illuminating and encouraging criticism of *my* book I wish to thank my friends Michael Hancher and George T. Wright, who took time from *their* books to give mine such careful readings. I would also like to thank John Espey for catching my errors in the manuscript and for the comforting word that books on Pound are almost doomed to have misprints, as if in tribute to Pound's own texts. Lawrence Mitchell and Kent Bales helped this book along as only the chairmen of one's department can. Parker Johnson introduced me to computers, Ron Akehurst helped me with programming and Provençal, and Nan Knowlton took over on the computer to prepare the manuscript for the printer. Pauline Yu and Ted Huters lived next door long enough to help me through Pound's Chinese; I hope my many questions over the back fence were not a factor in their decision to buy a new house. Special thanks to Anthony

Zahareas, Co-director of the University of Minnesota Center for Humanistic Studies, who knew a thin man when he saw one.

Grants from the University of Minnesota McMillan Fund, Graduate School Research Fund, and the College of Liberal Arts enabled me to examine material at Hamilton College and the Yale University Library. Grants from the University Computer Center and an especially generous grant from the Center for Humanistic Studies enabled me to prepare the manuscript for publication. *Paideuma: A Journal of Ezra Pound Scholarship* has granted permission to reprint my article, "Pound and Blake on Hell."

For living, sometimes cheerfully, with *The Cantos*, in Minnesota, in England, in Austria, I must thank Peter and Nicholas Furia; I have tried to thank their mother in the dedication of this book and with the promise of a return to Venice, one of Ezra Pound's enthusiasms which she shares.

Lines of Transmission

In 1687, just as the Governor of New England was about to confiscate the royal charter of Connecticut, the lights went out in the Hartford Assembly and Thomas Wadsworth, Ezra Pound's ancestor, rescued the document and hid it in a hollow oak. As a boy, Pound was taken to see the famous tree, and years later he recalled "the Charter Oak in Connecticut" (74/447) from a Pisan prison camp where he was sent, as he saw it, for similarly trying to "save" the "Constitution" (79/486).[1] What Pound believed he and his ancestor were fighting was the "historical black-out," a universal conspiracy to destroy, suppress, and subvert vital documents, a black-out that had even expunged the story of "Capn. Wadsworth" from "the school books" (97/671). Pound found his suspicions confirmed by a letter that John Adams wrote to Thomas Jefferson, warning of a universal despotism that

> Wherever it has resided
> has never failed to destroy all records, memorials,
> all histories which it did not like, and to corrupt
> those it was cunning enough to preserve..... (33/160)

Even as he wrote, Adams suspected that his correspondence was being monitored, though he joked to Jefferson that posterity would pay no attention to their letters anyway.

In Pound's view, Adams's prophecy had come true. The Adams-Jefferson letters, which he considered a "shrine and a monument" of American culture, our first true literature, were largely ignored, even in the universities.[2] Also blacked-out were the diary of John Quincy Adams, the memoirs of Martin Van Buren, and the anti-Bank speeches of Senator Thomas Hart Benton. The writings of these and other Americans were available, if at all, only in expensive, ponderous editions while the ideas of Marx and Mao were condensed and widely disseminated in cheap pamphlets. Not only American documents, but important texts from other cultures—the charters of a non-usurious bank in Siena, Sir Edward Coke's interpretations of *Magna Charta*, and the Confucian classics—had been kept out of circulation by a conspiracy of professors, publishers, and priests.

The Cantos can be read as a counterconspiracy against this historical black-out, an attempt to recover and recirculate lost documents: ecclesiastical edicts, commission reports, municipal records, diary entries, judicial writs, parliamentary statutes, contracts, mandates, treaties, log books, legislative codes, and regulations governing that most pervasive document of all, money. At one point Pound even incorporates the charter that Thomas Wadsworth had preserved in a Connecticut oak:

> Charles, God's Grace, '62
>   Brewen, Canfield,
>   a Body politique
>   and meere mocion
> Ordeyned, heirs, successors, Woollcott, Talcot, perpetual
> Seal, Governor, Deputy and 12 assistants
>   2nd. Thursday, May and October
> Oathes, Ship, transport and carry
>   under their common seal
> and not hinder fishinge
>   for salting
>   by Narrowgancett
> and on the South by the Sea
>   Mynes, Mynerals Precious Stones Quarries
>   As of our Mannor East Greenwich
>   in Soccage, not Capite
> One fifth of all oares Gold and Silver
>   23rd April, Westminster HOWARD   (109/773)

In part, Pound places this distilled charter into his poem the way a Cubist might stick a piece of newspaper into a collage, stressing its poetic cadences by cutting and juxtaposing, transforming as utilitarian an object as Marcel Duchamp's snowshovel or William Carlos Williams's red wheelbarrow by framing it in aesthetic space. Yet he also wants us to know the substance of the document, using *The Cantos* as his ancestor once used an oak tree, as an archive for texts he feared were threatened by the historical black-out.

The presence of such documents, like the "blubber" sections of *Moby Dick*, poses a major stumbling block for readers approaching *The Cantos* for the first time, as well as for critics trying to discern form and meaning in a poem that at one point includes eighty pages of extracts from John Adams's presidential papers and at another, a dozen pages taken from Byzantine guild regulations. It is not surprising that much criticism of *The Cantos* concentrates on the lyrical touchstones and regards this mass of documents as mere "ballast."[3] Indeed, Pound himself near the end of his life is said to have described his epic as a "botch" for precisely this reason: "I picked out this and that thing that interested me, and then jumbled them into a bag. But that's not the way to make a *work of art*."[4]

Until recently it has been difficult to treat this documentary rag-bag critically because Pound's "picking" and "jumbling" of his sources had not been traced. However, thanks to numerous scholars, working largely through the journal *Paideuma*, Pound's sources have been ferreted out, reprinted, and annotated.[5] Drawing on this scholarship, I wish to present an overview of Pound's use—artful and poetic use, I think—of historical documents in *The Cantos*. From this perspective, *The Cantos* emerge in a light different from that presented in most other critical studies; Pound's poem becomes, to borrow a phrase J. Hillis Miller has applied to *Bleak House*, a "document about documents," a "palimpsest," as Pound finally came to call it, overwritten with layer after layer of those texts whose creation, transmission, and translation constitute history.[6]

Such an approach emphasizes what is most traditional and what is most contemporary about *The Cantos*. When Pound called the epic a "poem including history," he was going back to the original function of epic as a tribal archive.[7] The oral poet who catalogued, updated, and transmitted the key documents of his culture was as much a defender of his tribe's identity as the hero whose martial deeds he celebrated. In *The Cantos* the heroes *are* the archivists—men like Kung, Coke, and an army of scholars, editors, and translators who preserve and "make new" the important documents of the past in palimpsests that mirror *The Cantos* themselves. It is these second- and thirdhand documents about documents, rather than original texts, that Pound recasts, emphasizing not only the document itself but the process of documentary transmission. That process, in turn, touches upon our own age's concern with the storage, retrieval, and dissemination of information. My own emphasis on this dimension of *The Cantos* reflects the fact that much of my research was conducted on a computer. What began as merely a technological aid gradually illuminated Pound's epic as the record of a struggle to preserve, process, and transmit documents.

By concentrating on its documentary bulk, moreover, we can better see the deeply conservative character of *The Cantos*, a conservatism that has its affinities with Pound's politics. The whole project of preserving and updating documents, for example, is conservative by definition, but Pound's attitude toward his documents is even more profoundly reactionary. In the document, he believed, he had the key to historical truth, provided he could get beyond the written text to the speaking voices buried beneath it. As poet, his task was to resurrect those dead voices and let them speak again to the present age.

Whatever shudders this view of writing, speaking, and repetition may generate among contemporary literary theorists, it does seem to have shaped Pound's enterprise.[8] On the one hand, it deepened the paranoia he felt over a historical black-out that could silence his voice—and texts—as it had buried others; on the other hand, it fired the evangelist and propagandist in him. If he could transmit—in "documentary" poetry, in haranguing prose, and, finally, over the radio—the lost documents from our past, he could help to transform his age just as medieval Europe was reborn when a flood of long-lost classical documents was channeled through the new technology of printing.

Canto 1 is about one of the products of that processing of documents—a Latin translation of *The Odyssey* by the Renaissance scholar Andreas Divus, published at the Paris printshop of Wechelus in 1538. Pound came across this book in "1906, 1908, or 1910" as he was browsing in a Paris bookstall.[9] Had he had a few more francs, he tells us, he could also have purchased Divus's *Iliad* and thus had editions of two works he considered "shored relics" from an ancient and advanced culture.[10] Homer's epics were themselves repositories of even older tales that Homer, working largely from "second-hand information," wove into unified narratives.[11] Behind these oral tales, moreover, were still older rites and myths that documented vital moments in a tribal past as precisely as "annals in a parish register."[12]

One such rite was the *nekuia*, or descent into the underworld, and Homer's recasting of this "pervasively archaic document"[13] in Book Eleven of *The Odyssey* makes it far "older" than the rest of the epic.[14] The fact that Homer is himself retelling an older story is an instance of what Pound called the "repeat" in history—not just history as a sequence of similar events but history *as* repetition, as the gathering, transmitting, and "making new" of documents from the past. The first word in *The Cantos*, "And," continues, rather than begins, an endless chain of textual repetition that links Pound to Divus and Homer and Odysseus, who himself is retelling the story of his underworld visit to King Alcinoüs. That story, in turn, reflects Pound's own descent into an archival past whose wisdom, like that of Tiresias, can regenerate the present. As Hugh Kenner has shown, Odysseus' shedding of sheep's blood so that the ghosts could drink and speak is a metaphor for the act of translation itself, whereby a living poet lends his voice to the dead.[15]

Similarly, the appearance of Anticlea breaks off Odysseus' dialogue with Tiresias just as Pound's illusion of original speech with Homer is broken by the intrusion of Andreas Divus, who will not "Lie quiet" but forces Pound to the grudging admission that all this aura of primitive origins is mediated by a book, a translation whose title page stands between us and the specter of the very past it conjures up. Pound could have translated Homer's original Greek, but by translating Divus's Latin translation he was emphasizing the many historical and textual layers between us and the nekuia, layers of repetition that stretch from gestural rite through oral tale to written manuscript to printed book, then back again through a modern poem.

Divus's translation registers one of the most important of those repetitions, for Divus designed his *Odyssey* as a practical guide, a "pony" to help sixteenth-century schoolboys and scholars make contact with the ancient classical texts that entered western Europe after the fall of Constantinople. It was this resurrection of ancient documents, Pound believed, that sparked the Renaissance, and he hoped that renewed contact with such archaic sources could regenerate modern society. By giving the date and place of publication of Divus's *Odyssey*, Pound footnotes the coincidental recovery of Greek texts with western Europe's adaptation of the Chinese technology of printing—a coincidence of texts and process that allowed for the quick dissemination of important documents. In Canto 30 Pound will illustrate the same coincidence with another document, a letter from the printer Hieronymous Soncinus to his patron Caesare Borgia:

> ...and here have I brought cutters of letters
> and printers not vile and vulgar
> (in Fano Caesaris)
> notable and sufficient compositors
> and a die-cutter for greek fonts and hebrew
> named Messire Francesco da Bologna
> not only of the usual types but he hath excogitated
> a new form called cursive or chancellry letters   (30/148)

It was the creation of such new "greek fonts" that allowed for the printing of books like Divus's, making classical texts available to ever-increasing numbers of people. However, the promise of printing quickly soured, in Pound's view, and in Cantos 14 and 15 he compares hell itself to a vast "printing-house" that effectively buries the really important cultural documents in a welter of worthless print typified by the daily newspaper. Pound did, after all, come across Divus's *Odyssey* at the bottom of a heap of cheap books in a Paris stall.

What he celebrates in Divus's translation, however, is its power to erase itself as printed text and render the nekuia in something like its original spoken form. In his article "Translators of Greek" Pound used the nekuia passage as a litmus test for various Renaissance translations of *The Odyssey* and praised Andreas Divus for his skill in breaking through the printed word and into song.[16] Such an achievement, Pound believed, registered the grafting of classical culture, renewed through Renaissance Latin, onto the native lyric poetry of medieval Europe. The joining of these two traditions marked a crucial juncture in the history of poetry, and Pound captures that merger by rendering Divus's Latin *Odyssey* in the rhythm, syntax, and alliterative verse of Anglo-Saxon poetry:

> Souls stained with recent tears, girls tender,
> Men many, mauled with bronze lance heads,
> Battle spoil, bearing yet dreory arms...   (1/3-4)

Through this highly literary primitivism, Pound documents the merger of classical and medieval traditions and recaptures the sense of primal speech behind the printed text.

The opposition between printed text and spoken word will occupy Pound throughout *The Cantos*, and at the end of Canto 1 he contrasts Divus's lyrical translation of *The Odyssey* with a pedantic translation of the Homeric Hymns into Latin by a "Cretan" (Pound intends the pun) named Georgius Dartona. The Hymns were not really composed by Homer but by the Homeridae, bards who preserved Homer's epics in oral performances and added these lyrics to their repertoire. Like *The Iliad* and *The Odyssey*, the Hymns survived at Constantinople until the Eastern Empire fell and then were smuggled into western Europe. The printer who composed Divus's *Odyssey* also included Dartona's Latin translations of the Homeric Hymns in the back of his volume, and these "Literary documents of great antiquity"[17] forge another link in the chain of textual transmission binding the past to the present.

By retranslating fragments from the "Cretan's" translations of the Hymns to Aphrodite, Pound is trying to recapture the same poetic splendor Divus transmitted from Homer, a splendor symbolized by the goddess herself, eternally reborn through generations of textual metamorphoses. For the first seven Cantos Pound follows Aphrodite's transformations in literary documents that carry him through Greece, Rome, Spain, Provence, and Tuscany. By retracing these lines of transmission, he tries to resurrect Aphrodite's buried beauty in texts that, like those of Andreas Divus and Sir James Frazer, will serve as a "golden bough" to restore our contact with the fertile underworld of history.

In the order of the Homeric Hymns established by their first printing in 1488, the Hymns to Aphrodite are followed by a Hymn to Dionysus, and Pound follows that same order as he moves from Canto 1 to Canto 2. This time, however, he traces a different line of textual transmission between ancient Greece and Renaissance Europe—a line that leads through Ovid, whose *Metamorphoses* was an encyclopedic palimpsest that helped to preserve classical myths in western Europe through the Middle Ages. Pound recasts Ovid's retelling of the Hymn to Dionysus, in which the god, disguised as a young boy, seeks passage on a ship to Naxos, a center for his cults. When the sailors try to sell him into slavery, Dionysus transforms them into dolphins and the ship into a grape arbor:

God-sleight then, god-sleight:
   Ship stock fast in sea-swirl
Ivy upon the oars, King Pentheus,
   grapes with no seed but sea-foam   (2/7)

Just as the nekuia of Canto 1 was a metaphor for Pound's own descent into ancient texts, here the story of metamorphosis reflects its own textual transformations. When Ovid retold these Homeric Hymns, he used a narrator who himself "retold" the story, a device that mirrored the layers of transmission and metamorphosis that lay between Ovid and his original. Pound uses the same device when he retells Ovid's retelling: the story of Dionysus' metamorphosis is being told by one of the sailors, Acoetes, to King Pentheus in order to convert—metamorphose—the king, who had been persecuting the Dionysian sects. By translating Ovid's translation, Pound seeks to make the Latin poet new after many years of neglect by nineteenth-century poets and readers, perhaps with the hope that Ovid could again transfuse poetry as he had in the Middle Ages through Arthur Golding's translation, to which Pound alludes by adapting Golding's "Schoeny" for the name of Atalanta's father (2/6).

Thus, Canto 2 incorporates another palimpsest of literary documents whose layers trace the metamorphic passage of poetic beauty, symbolized by Aphrodite, from ancient Greece to medieval Europe.

Seal sports in the spray-whited circles of cliff-wash,
Sleek head, daughter of Lir,
   eyes of Picasso
Under black fur-hood, lithe daughter of Ocean;
And the wave runs in the beach-groove:
"Eleanor, ἐλέναυς and ἐλέπτολις !"   (2/6)

The foam-born goddess who emerged from Divus's translation here changes first into the seal-daughter of a Celtic sea-god, then into the seal-eyed women of Picasso's portraits, from there into the city- and man-destroying Helen of Troy, and finally into the equally destructive Eleanor of Aquitaine. Eleanor leads to the next link in Pound's chain of textual transmission, the troubadours of Provence, for whom Ovid's *Metamorphoses* was a crucial "document." The troubadour songs renewed Ovid's retold myths and transformed Aphrodite into a beloved lady whose beauty reflected the lyrical power of the song that embodied her.

Yet Ovid was not the only source for that song. The first troubadour, Guillaume Poictiers, grandfather of Eleanor of Aquitaine, "brought the song up out of Spain" (8/32) where the Arabs had preserved the Greek texts in

translation. It was through this Iberian source, as well as through Ovid, that
the troubadours of Provence maintained continuity with the classical world,
and in Canto 3 Pound retraces that line of transmission by translating a
fragment from the *Cantar de mio Cid.* The Cid, who "rode up to Burgos" (3/11),
is an obvious parallel to Odysseus, but he may also be seen as a figure for the
progression of the very song Guillaume brought "up out of Spain." In the
episode Pound translates, a little girl reads to the Cid from an edict that exiles
him from his native land:

> Una niña de nueve años,
> To the little gallery over the gate, between the towers,
> Reading the writ, voce tinnula:
> That no man speak to, feed, help Ruy Diaz,
> On pain to have his heart out, set on a pike spike
> And both his eyes torn out, and all his goods sequestered,
> "And here, Myo Cid, are the seals,
> The big seal and the writing."   (3/11)

As the little girl with "voce tinnula" defies the heavy writ by speaking to the
Cid, we find another clash between written document and spoken word, and
the black-out imposed on the Cid by this writ foreshadows the repression of
troubadour song, indeed of all Provençal culture, in the Church's Albigensian
Crusade.

That historical black-out was prompted by the Church's belief, which Pound
shared, that Provençal culture perpetuated pagan rites and myths. Although
that culture was destroyed in 1244 in the massacre at Mt. Ségur, the
troubadour songs, and the ancient myths they embodied, survived, first as oral
texts, then in written fragments smuggled into Italy where they were collected,
copied into illuminated manuscripts, and augmented with biographical *vidas*
and *razos* of the troubadours. Here, Pound believed, classical myths underwent
another metamorphosis, and in Cantos 4 and 5 he traced the textual
transformations that link Provence with the classical world.[18]

The first vida Pound translates, that of Guillems de Cabestanh, plays off the
threat of mutilation in the edict against the Cid. Cabestanh loved the lady
Soremonda, whose jealous husband cut out Cabestanh's heart and served it to
his wife. Upon learning she had eaten her lover's heart, Soremonda leapt to
her death:

> And she went toward the window and cast her down,
> > "All the while, the while, swallows crying: Ityn!
> > "It is Cabestan's heart in the dish."
> > "It is Cabestan's heart in the dish?
> > "No other taste shall change this."   (4/13)

This vida transforms Ovid's transformation of the Greek myth of Procne, who killed her son Itys and served him to her husband to avenge the rape of her sister Philomela. Pound weaves these textual layers together with a series of verbal metamorphoses, "'Tis. 'Tis. Ytis!" and—a gruesome pun on "eaten"—"Ityn, Ityn" (4/13-14). Ovid retold this myth in the *Metamorphoses*, where he described the transformation of Procne into a swallow—another pun that points back to the cannibalistic feast and to the "swallow crying" as Soremonda flies from the window (4/13). What fascinates Pound, again, is not so much the tale of metamorphosis as the metamorphosis of the tale, and he emphasizes the continuity of troubadour song with pagan myth by describing the wind that catches Soremonda in her swallowlike leap as "out of Rhodez" (4/13), a Provençal town (Rodez) that recalls Rhodes, site of the ancient cults supposedly perpetuated by the troubadours.

Having moved backwards from troubadour vida through Ovid and into Greek myth, Pound switches direction and starts with Greek myth and traces it forward through Ovid and into the life of another troubadour, Peire Vidal. Ovid's retelling of the myth of Actaeon, transformed into a stag and devoured by his own dogs after he glimpsed Diana bathing, resurfaces in Provence:

> Actaeon...
> > and a valley,
> The valley is thick with leaves, with leaves, the trees,
> The sunlight glitters, glitters a-top,
> Like a fish-scale roof,
> > Like the church roof in Poictiers
> If it were gold.   (4/14)

The textual metamorphosis is reflected in Pound's transformation of the sun-dappled leaves over Diana's bath into the glittering tiles of a church roof in Poitiers, fief of the first troubadour, Guillaume, duke of Aquitaine.

Into this multitextured setting, Pound introduces the troubadour Peire Vidal, walking through the forest reciting Ovid:

> Then Actaeon: Vidal,
> Vidal. It is old Vidal speaking,
> > stumbling along in the wood,
> Not a patch, not a lost shimmer of sunlight,
> > the pale hair of the goddess.
> . . . .
> > The dogs leap on Actaeon.
> Stumbling, stumbling along in the wood,
> Muttering, muttering Ovid.   (4/14-15)

Dressed in wolf-skins to woo a lady named LaLoba (the wolf), Vidal reincarnates the mythical figure of Actaeon and, like his prototype, is nearly killed by a pack of hunting dogs. In a dizzying series of metamorphoses, Pound weaves back and forth among other classical myths, Ovidian tales, and troubadour vidas, to create an intricate palimpsest of overlapping texts mirrored by that "fish-scale roof" in Poitiers. Another metaphor for Pound's poem is the pool of rippling water whose spreading rings reflect the concentric versions of the same myths told and retold through various ages and cultures.

> "Pergusa…pool…pool…Gargaphia,
> "Pool…pool of Salmacis."   (4/15)

In these lines from Ovid, the pools themselves metamorphose into one another—Gargaphia, where Diana splashed Actaeon to transform him into a stag; Pergusa, where Hades abducted Persephone; and Salmacis, where Hermaphroditus and Salmacis were turned into androgynes. Pound then transforms these Ovidian pools into a Japanese brook whose "film" carries "white petals" under the "Tree of the Visages!" (4/15). This image, in turn, spills over into a twentieth-century cinematic metaphor, as "visages" modulates to "Adige, thin film of images" (4/16).

The Adige is a river in Italy, a metamorphosis of the Provençal river Garonne, and the geographical shift from Provence to Italy parallels the next great metamorphosis of texts, as troubadour song is "made new" in the Tuscan poetry of Cavalcanti and Dante. The troubadour poet Arnaut Daniel is a pivotal figure in this line of transmission, and Pound quotes his celebration of a universal Neoplatonic light that ripples like endlessly flowing water: "Thus the light rains, thus pours, *e lo soleills plovil*" (4/15). At the end of Canto 4 this metaphor for textual metamorphosis is itself metamorphosed into the concentric walls of Ecbatan and the Roman arena at Vernoa.

At the center of those rings is Eleanor of Aquitaine—her name itself defines her as a metamorphosis of Helen of Troy—and in Canto 6 Pound traces her shuttlings among lovers and locales through a collage of prosaic documents. Her reputed affairs with her uncle Raymond, who "commanded in Acre" and "had known her in girlhood" (6/21), and with Saladin in Jordan, her divorce from Louis VII of France, and her marriage to Henry II of England are refracted through texts whose flat legalese understates and thus underscores the passions generated by this granddaughter of Duke Guillaume, "Seventh of Poitiers, Ninth of Aquitain."

> Nauphal, Vexis, Harry joven
> In pledge for all his life and life of all his heirs
> Shall have Gisors, and Vexis, Neufchastel
> But if no issue Gisors shall revert…   (6/21)

By this contract, Louis' daughter Margaret would marry "young Henry," the son of Eleanor and Henry II, and Margaret's dowry would include the disputed Norman Vexin. But when young Henry died heirless, Eleanor and Henry II refused to adhere to the stipulation that the territory revert to Louis. The conflict was eased by another agreement that bestowed the Vexin upon another of Louis' daughters, Alix, who was then betrothed to Henry and Eleanor's son Richard. But when Alix went to live in England as the ward of her uncle, Henry seduced her, and Richard refused to go through with the marriage.

> "Need not wed Alix...in the name
> Trinity holy indivisible...Richard our brother
> Need not wed Alix once his father's ward and...
> But whomso he choose...for Alix, etc... (6/22)

It took this document to release Richard from his contract, and its ellipses hint at the passions and violence generated by women like Eleanor and Alix.

Such women also inspire poetry, and Pound contrasts these prosaic documents with a song addressed to Eleanor by Bernart de Ventadorn. The troubadour tells Eleanor of his beloved "Lady of Ventadour," whose jealous husband imprisoned her and banished Bernart. Bernart took refuge at Poitiers, where Eleanor herself had come after her divorce from Louis, and there he wrote his lament for his lady whose imprisonment foreshadowed Eleanor's fate in England. Once again, the text reflects its own history, and when Pound says that Eleanor "spoiled in a British climate" (7/24), he is thinking of the lyrical power embodied by the women celebrated in troubadour song. Although that beauty left Provence and only "spoiled" in England, it was reborn in Tuscany in the poetry of Cavalcanti and Dante. Pound traces that shift by translating Cavalcanti's translation of Bernart's plea to Eleanor to "free" his lady, who, like the song she embodies, "sheds such light in the air" (6/22).

In Canto 6 the metamorphosis of troubadour song into Tuscan poetry is registered by another document—Cunizza da Romano's deed of manumission:

> Cunizza, da Romano,
> That freed her slaves on a Wednesday
> Masnatas et servos, witness
> Picus de Farinatis
> and Don Elinus and Don Lipus
>   sons of Farinato de' Farinati
> "free of person, free of will"
> "free to buy, witness, sell, testate." (6/22-23)

Like Eleanor of Aquitaine and Bernart's Lady of Ventadour, Cunizza was herself imprisoned for her love of the troubadour Sordello, but in this document she frees slaves she inherited from her brother and father. In *Guide to Kulchur* Pound celebrates this prosaic document, which we know only from a thirteenth-century copy in the Treviso archives: "There was nothing in Chréstien de Troyes' narratives, nothing in Rimini or in the tales of the antients to surpass the facts of Cunizza, with, in her old age, great kindness, thought for her slaves."[19] What Pound implies here is that just as the *fact* of Cunizza's gesture of forgiveness is more romantic than anything in fiction, so the raw document itself is more poetic, particularly as he renders its cadences and phrases, than any romance.

This deed of manumission not only frees slaves but inspires the flight of song from Provence to Tuscany. Another extract reveals that when Cunizza signed the document, she was staying

> In the house of the Cavalcanti
>   anno 1265:
> Free go they all as by full manumission
> All serfs of Eccelin my father da Romano
> Save those who were with Alberic at Castra San Zeno
> And let them go also
> The devils of hell in their body.   (29/142)

In *Guide to Kulchur* Pound pictures "Cunizza. white-haired in the House of the Cavalcanti, Dante, small gutter-snipe, or small boy hearing the talk in his father's kitchen, or, later, from Guido, of beauty incarnate."[20] Even in old age she embodies the metamorphic beauty incarnate in Aphrodite, Helen, and Eleanor, and here she transmits it to Guido Cavalcanti and Dante. These Tuscan poets, in turn, will transform that beauty again, Guido in "*Donna mi prega*," which Pound himself will "make new" in Canto 36, and Dante in a paradise peopled by beautiful women like Beatrice and Cunizza herself.

In Canto 7 Pound recapitulates the entire process of textual transmission he has traced in these early Cantos.

> Eleanor (she spoiled in a British climate)
> "Ελανδρος and Ἑλέπτολις , and
> poor old Homer blind,
> blind as a bat,
> Ear, ear for the sea-surge;
>   rattle of old men's voices.
> And then the phantom Rome,
>   marble narrow for seats

"Si pulvis nullus" said Ovid,
"Erit, nullum tamen excute."
Then file and candles, e li mestiers ecoutes;
Scene for the battle only, but still scene,
Pennons and standards y cavals armatz
Not mere succession of strokes, sightless narration,
And Dante's "ciocco," brand struck in the game.   (7/24)

Beginning with the punning identification of Eleanor and Helen, he retraces the metamorphoses of poetic beauty from "poor old Homer" through "phantom Rome," where Ovid advises lovers to use the narrow seats of the arena for foreplay; then to Spain with the Cid's "Pennons and standards"; from there to Provence via the troubadour fragment "y cavals armatz"; and, finally, to Tuscany and "Dante's 'ciocco.'"

This lyrical beauty is transmitted to modern poets through the precise prose of Flaubert and the "weighted motion" of Henry James's "endless sentence." James himself appears as Tiresias, a "phantom" with "great domed head," "drinking the tone of things" as Tiresias drank the blood shed by Odysseus. James is Pound's link to the poetic past, his lyrical prose a golden bough to a young American expatriate "seeking for buried beauty" (7/25). Thus, Pound's odyssey to renew his contact with an ancient line of textual transmission is recast as a Jamesian thriller—"The Aspern Papers" or "The Jolly Corner"— with Pound "Knocking at empty rooms" and probing "for old wills" (7/27) in a melodramatic search for secret documents.

To recapture the beauty buried in these ancient texts, Pound, like Divus, must break through the "pasteboard partitions" of the printed book into the sound of the human voice. But, as he found when he tried to make Divus "lie quiet," the printed page impedes his grasp of the very splendor it reveals: "Damn the partition! Paper, dark brown and stretched, / Flimsy and damned partition" (7/25). All he can present are fragmentary relics—Homer's description of Helen's beauty, Golding's sumptuous translation of Ovid's Atalanta, and Arnaut Daniel's celebration of his beloved Lady of Bouvila—where the dead voices can speak again. Yet, through such "shored" and "shelved" fragments (8/28), Pound can enter into the past and document the metamorphoses of a poetic beauty he glimpsed as Aphrodite at the end of Divus's Odyssey, retracing the lines of its transmission from the ancient world and making it new, again, in the present.

II

Malatesta's Post-Bag

In Cantos 8 through 11 Pound rewove a "rag-bag" of historical documents—letters, memoirs, treaties, bills of lading, ecclesiastical edicts—in order to redeem a fifteenth-century condottiere, Sigismundo Malatesta of Rimini, from the historical black-out. Pound saw that Malatesta stood at the point where a recovered classical past promised to revitalize western Europe, and he portrayed the Lord of Rimini as a major conduit for that cultural transmission. To most historians, however, Sigismundo was a ruthless barbarian with an inexplicable taste for art—an impression based largely on the *Commentaries* of Pope Pius II, one of Malatesta's fiercest enemies. To counter that image, Pound combed Italian archives and libraries for memoirs, correspondence, and other documents about Sigismundo, but he also used a secondhand source, a romantic biography by Charles Yriarte that reprinted crucial documents in an appendix.[1] Pound drew upon this palimpsest, as well as on documents he examined first-hand in Siena and Rimini, believing "that documents, personal letters and what not proved one thing. A letter proved what the bloke who wrote it wanted the receiver to believe on the day he wrote it. The rest of history has to be derived from computation." In the Malatesta Cantos Pound derived Sigismundo through a "critical reading of the chief primary sources" and showed that "long after the 'facts' have receded into a past from which they cannot be directly recalled, the voices of the actors can still . . . be heard in the documents."[2]

To bring those voices back to life from dead documents, Pound resurrects one of Malatesta's letters, written to Giovanni Medici in 1449 from Cremona, where Malatesta was bogged down in a siege:

> *Frater tamquam*
> *Et compater carissime: tergo*
> *. . .hanni de*
> *. . .dicis*
> *. . .entia*

Equivalent to:
>   Giohanni of the Medici,
>   Florence.   (8/28)

Pound duplicates the back ("tergo") side of the letter where the address is partially obscured by Sigismundo's elegant wax seal. The seal itself is significant, for it was designed by Pisanello and represented, for Pound, "the thoroughness of Rimini's civilization" in the mid-fifteenth century.[3] The act of reconstructing what lies under the seal thus becomes another metaphor for Pound's struggle to recover a lost age and its obscured hero.

The imaginative breaking of the seal also establishes a key documentary motif, for the letter deals with the first of many broken contracts that will plague Malatesta's career and finally destroy him. Here Malatesta urges Giovanni Medici to press for peace in the War of the Milanese Succession, where Florence, Venice, Francesco Sforza, and King Alphonso of Naples and Aragon ("Ragona") were fighting for the dukedom of Milan. Malatesta had originally been hired as a condottiere by King Alphonso but then broke his contract to sign on with the Venice-Florence alliance. The king's outrage persisted long after peace was made and finally helped to bring Malatesta down—a fall that Pound pictures as a metamorphosis of Odysseus' descent, where a good man goes down "among the duds" of his age, or, like Actaeon, is dragged down by dogs.

With Odyssean *polumetis* (many-mindedness), however, Malatesta can turn from his siege of Sforza's army to the construction of his architectural triumph, the Tempio Malatestiano at Rimini. For Pound, the Tempio, while a "jumble and a junk-shop" like his own *Cantos*, "nevertheless" stands as a monument to Sigismundo, a "failure worth all the successes of his age."[4] In his letter to Giovanni Medici, Sigismundo tries to direct construction on the Tempio from a battlefield, and Pound uses the document to establish his hero as a generous patron who understands the artists he has hired, promising the "Maestro di pentore," Piero della Francesca, not only the commission of painting frescoes for the Tempio but a lifetime of artistic freedom to "work as he likes, / Or waste his time as he likes" (8/29)— an elegant artistic contract that plays off of the devious contracts that engulf Malatesta himself.

Pound then cuts back to those political contracts with excerpts from other letters. In 1450 Sforza took over Milan, and Florence broke its alliance with Venice to make a treaty with the new duke. Venice, in turn, joined forces with Alphonso of Aragon, and when the king invaded Tuscany in 1452, Florence hired Malatesta to defend the city. In these musical-chair alliances Malatesta suddenly became an ally of Sforza, the "aforesaid most illustrious / Duke of Milan," whom he had been fighting just a few years before. To underscore these dizzying shifts, Pound throws in fragments that record how once before

Sforza and Malatesta had been allies when Francesco and his new bride Bianca (who led the forces that Malatesta besieged at Cremona!) stopped at Rimini "For two day's pleasure" before heading "to the wars southward" (8/31).

Still another turnabout comes in an earlier contract:

> With the interruption:
>> *Magnifico, compater et carissime*
>> (Johanni di Cosimo)
> Venice has taken me on again
>> At 7,000 a month, *fiorini di Camera*.   (8/30)

Although this letter was written a month before the one that opened Canto 8, Pound places it here to emphasize the bewildering shifts of alliance that undermine Malatesta's world: it completes a circle of contracts by which Sigismundo has been ally and enemy of Venice, Florence, Sforza, and Alphonso of Aragon.

By cutting to an unpublished manuscript he had found in the Gambalunga Library at Rimini, Pound raises another voice from the dead, one that gives a different view of Malatesta and his broken contracts. Gaspare Broglio, one of Malatesta's soldiers, provided a bitterly partisan view of his chieftain in his *Cronaca*, and Pound interweaves the colloquial voice of this memoir with the stiff officialese of other documents, highlighting Broglio's slangy references to Sigismundo's enemies like "Feddy" Urbino, "Pio" (Pius II), and "Wattle" Sforza. The *Cronaca's* quick shifts and whirling summaries, moreover, reflect the protean energy of Malatesta himself.

> And old Sforza bitched us at Pesaro;
>> (*sic*) March the 16th:
> "that Messire Alessandro Sforza
>> is become lord of Pesaro
> through the wangle of the Illus. Sgr. Mr. Fedricho d'Orbino
> Who worked the wangle with Galeaz
>> through the wiggling of Messer Francesco,
> Who waggled it so that Galeaz should sell Pesaro
>> to Alex and Fossembrone to Feddy;
> and he hadn't the right to sell.
> And this he did *bestialmente*; that is Sforza did *bestialmente*
> as he had promised him, Sigismundo, *per capitoli*
>> to see that he, Malatesta, should have Pesaro"   (9/34-35)

Broglio's angry voice here chokes on another broken contract—one that double-crossed his boss. In 1442 Sigismundo agreed to help Francesco Sforza wage war in the Marches of Ancona; in return, Sforza pledged to help

Malatesta take the town of Pesaro from Galeazzo Malatesta, Sigismundo's cousin. However, Sforza, with the help of Federigo Urbino, struck a bargain with Galeazzo and purchased Pesaro for 20,000 florins in 1445, arranging a marriage between his brother, Alessandro Sforza, and Galeazzo's niece. The deal also involved the sale of Fossembrone, another holding of the Malatesta family, to Federigo Urbino.

Broglio's word for all of this double-dealing is *bestialmente*, a soldier's invective for buggery and back-stabbing, and he deepens the overtones of sexual perversion by describing the treachery of "Feddy," "Alex," and the others as "working the wangle," "wiggling," and "waggling it." When Broglio turns to Sigismundo's own breach of contract with Alphonso of Aragon, however, he glosses it over as a mere "traditio"—a changeover:

> And the King o' Ragona, Alphonse le roy d'Aragon,
> > was the next nail in our coffin,
> And all you can say is, anyway,
> that he Sigismundo called a town council
> And Valturio said "as well for a sheep as a lamb
> > and this change-over (*haec traditio*)
> As old bladder said: "*rem eorum saluavit*"
> Saved the Florentine state; and that, maybe, was something.
> And "Florence our natural ally" as they said in the meeting
> > for whatever that was worth afterward.   (9/35)

What Broglio describes here is the town meeting Sigismundo called in Rimini after he had broken his contract with Alphonso of Aragon and hired on with the Venetian-Florentine alliance. The enraged Alphonso demanded that the advance money he had given Sigismundo be returned, and Broglio quotes the tough advice of Roberto Valturio, who said that, since Alphonso was going to be angry anyway over the breach of contract, Malatesta might as well keep the money instead of trying to appease the king by sheepishly returning it. Broglio then adds more whitewash to his account by quoting the Rimini council's rationalization that Florence was a more "natural" ally of Rimini than Aragon. Even the voice of Malatesta's enemy, Pope Pius II, whom Broglio nicknames "Pio" and "old bladder," gets pulled into Sigismundo's defense, grudgingly admitting that Malatesta's "traditio" had saved the Florentine state.

Through Broglio's *Cronaca* we see Malatesta's greatest military triumph, the defeat of a vastly larger papal army at the battle of Vitelleschi in 1461. On the eve of the battle Sigismundo addresses his troops:

> All I want you to do is to follow the orders,
> They've got a bigger army,
> > but there are more men in this camp.   (10/47)

Sigismundo's joke here is that there were a lot of papal legates in the opposing army and, by implication therefore, a lot of homosexuals. As he speaks, an eagle lights on his pole and Malatesta quips, "The Romans would have called that an augury." The classic pose casts Malatesta as a conduit for the regeneration of the ancient world in Renaissance Italy.

The other side of that classical figure, however, is a Malatesta "a bit too POLUMETIS" (9/36) in his Odyssean shifts of allegiance among warring factions. Broglio's account of his commander's narrow escape in 1447 from an ambush by a neighboring condottiere makes him seem more like a beleaguered Actaeon:

> Down here in the marsh they trapped him
> > in one year,
> And he stood in the water up to his neck
> > to keep the hounds off him,
> And he floundered about in the marsh
> > and came in after three days,
> That was Astorre Manfredi of Faenza
> > who worked the ambush
> > and set the dogs off to find him,
> In the marsh, down here under Mantua.   (9/34)

Like Napoleon, who discovered "The fifth element: mud" (34/166), Malatesta is bogged down in the muck of his age: in his escape from the ambush, he vainly appeals to a supposed ally, "Carlo Gonzaga sitting like a mud-frog," (10/42); later he is forced to "set up bombards in muck" (9/37) to besiege a castle; and, finally, he is dragged down by "the whole lump lot" (10/45) of his enemies.

Among those enemies were the Sienese, with whom Malatesta had broken another contract. In 1454, after peace was finally made among the city-states fighting for control of Milan, Sigismundo hired on with Siena in its skirmish with Count Orsini of Pitigliano. Malatesta took one of the count's castles, but, instead of pressing the siege, he struck a truce with Orsini without consulting the commune of Siena. The Sienese were outraged and tried to arrest Sigismundo, but he broke camp and fled, leaving behind his equipment and baggage, including his post-bag filled with letters. The letters lay unnoticed in the Sienese archives until they were accidentally discovered in the nineteenth century. Yriarte reprints some of the letters in the appendix to his book on Malatesta, but Pound also examined the documents firsthand. In Canto 9 he recasts eight of the letters, cutting them up into a collage of texts that crisscross and overlap to give another view of Malatesta's hectic many-mindedness. Pound recreates the feel of the texts as he flips from letter to letter—skimming such weighty salutations as *"Magnifice ac potens domine"*; *"Magnifico exso.*

Signor Mio"; *"Illustre signor mio"*; and *"Malatesta de Malatestis ad Magnificum Dominuum Patremque suum"*—much as Malatesta himself must have perused the well-worn letters during his long encampment.

The first letters deal with the construction of the Tempio, which Sigismundo, again, is trying to direct from the battlefield. The Tempio was designed by Leon Battista Alberti, but when he was called to Rome, the workmen were confused by the plans and Sigismundo had to bring in another architect, Matteo Nuti. What made the plans so tricky was that Alberti was building the Tempio around the shell of the old Church of San Francesco, and Nuti writes to let Sigismundo know that he has gone over them with the construction foreman, "master Alwidge" (9/37). Suddenly Nuti's letter is interrupted with "JHesus"; the word actually comes from another letter in the post-bag, but Pound's arrangement makes it seem like it is Malatesta's exasperated outcry over the construction delay. His frustration could only have increased when he received this second letter, for it comes from "master Alwidge's" son Giovane, who reports that his father has shown the troublesome plans to Sigismundo's chancellor, "Mr. Genare" (9/38), but still is confused. Young Giovane then takes it upon himself to suggest that he "shud go to rome to talk to mister Albert so as I can no what he thinks about it rite." The transparency of Giovane's desire for a trip to Rome leaks through his Huck Finn grammar and spelling—as does his smugness at being able to do his illiterate father's reading and writing.

From architectural plans, we progress to the shipment of building materials as Pound cuts to the third letter in the Sienese post-bag, from the artist and medallist Matteo di Pasti:

> *"Illustre signor mio*, Messire Battista..."
>
> "First: Ten slabs best red, seven by 15, by one third,
> Eight ditto, good red, 15 by three by one.
> "Six of same, 15 by one by one.
> Eight columns 15 by three and one third
>   etc...with carriage, danars 151   (9/38)

As if to mimic Malatesta's own perusal of this letter, Pound glances from the salutation, where Pasti notes he has received Alberti's plans for the façade of the Tempio, right to the body of the letter, where Pasti quotes a contract with his brother, a stone merchant from Verona, for the marble.

With the Tempio going up, Pound turns to the next letter, which he renders from Yriarte's French translation, concerning an appropriately Gallic subject— Sigismundo's affair with a young girl, "Sr. Galeazzo's daughter" (9/38). Malatesta's secretary writes to report that Isotta degli Atti, Sigismundo's "regular" mistress and soon-to-be third wife, has learned of the affair. When

Isotta confronted the girl, however, the young wench staunchly "denied the whole matter and kept her end up without losing her temper" (9/38). This letter at first seems to cut away from the Tempio until we learn that Sigismundo dedicated the Tempio to Isotta; as it stands, however, the letter debunks some of the idealism that might surround such a dedication and reminds us that Sigismundo's many-mindedness—like that of Odysseus—extended not only to war but to love. The secretary, who signs the letter "D. de M," goes on to compliment Malatesta on his capture of Sorano—a compliment that must have rankled the Sienese when they went through the post-bag. The closing, "Everyone wants to be remembered to you" (9/38), is quite funny in light of the squabbling going on in Malatesta's household in his absence. These last images reinforce the comic parallel between Sigismundo and Odysseus, for while Malatesta made a breach in the walls of a besieged city, he did not enter and conquer it, and his household troubles are caused not by raucous suitors but by his own indiscretions.

Pound keeps construction of the Tempio in view as he interjects another snippet from the second letter, from "master Alwidge's" eager son Giovane, mentioning that Sagramoro, one of Malatesta's counselors, was about "to put up the derricks" (9/38) for the Tempio's façade. Pound then creates another documentary rhyme by juxtaposing this letter from his foreman's son with a letter about his own son Sallustio. The letter comes from "Lunarda da Palla" (9/39), Sallustio's tutor, and informs Malatesta how much the boy enjoys the pony that Malatesta has sent him. Even as he reports this pleasant news, however, da Palla adds still more home-front troubles for Sigismundo to worry about—a botched job on Isotta's garden wall by a stone mason whose name Pound renders in English as "Rambottom" to suggest the trouble he is giving the family in Malatesta's Odyssean absence. More fragments from earlier letters by Nuti and Pasti about work on the Tempio only intensify the closing phrase of da Palla's letter that "noboddy hear can do anything without you" (9/39) and suggest that Sigismundo's failure to press the siege of Sorano may well have reflected these domestic problems. Those problems are offset by a letter from Sallustio, thanking his "Magnificent and Exalted Lord and Father in especial my lord" (9/39) for the gift of the pony. Sallustio's stiff prose contrasts with the colloquial styles of the preceding letters, yet registers, beneath its formality, the boy's affection for his father.

Pound shrewdly follows this innocent letter with a phrase from another letter that must have made the Sienese explode:

"ILLUSTRIOUS PRINCE:
   "Unfitting as it is that I should offer counsels to Hannibal…"   (9/40)

The letter comes from Malatesta's court poet, Servulus Trajatus, who subtly urges Malatesta to take control of politically-torn Siena instead of merely working as its condottiere. Trajatus carefully prefaces his recommendation with an apology that he, a poet, should offer advice to a military leader as great as Hannibal.

The final letter Pound uses from the Sienese post-bag comes from Petrus Genariis, another of Sigismundo's secretaries, who reports on the arrival of the shipment of marble described in Matteo di Pasti's letter. Genariis explains how he got ahold of the marble from authorities in Ferrara who had impounded it against the debts of the captain. The captain had fled, leaving ship and cargo behind, so Genariis paid the debts, got the marble, and is holding the boat until the captain returns and reimburses him. The letter indicates that at least somebody back in Rimini can do something in Malatesta's absence, and it provides a parallel to Malatesta's flight from Sorano, where he, like the dunned captain, left his post-bag and equipment behind.

Genariis includes news about the progression of work on the Tempio, which has been delayed by bad weather, and about the difficulty of obtaining elephant sculptures to support the columns. The marble elephants are fitting emblems for a fifteenth-century metamorphosis of Hannibal, whose Tempio constitutes an architectural act of remembering the classical past and grafting it onto the Renaissance. Like the great classical library his brother Novello built in Cesena to hold Greek and Latin manuscripts, the Tempio Malatestiano is itself an architectural document, one that "registers a concept"—a record of "what one man has embodied in the last 1000 years of the occident."[5] The many layers of this stone palimpsest wind as far back into the classical past as Divus's *Odyssey*. On its site there had been a temple for the worship of Venus which, during Christian times, was converted to a chapel for the Virgin called "Santa Maria in Trivio" (9/36). Later, this chapel was rebuilt as the Gothic Church of San Francesco, and, since it contained the tombs of his ancestors, Sigismundo did not want the old church to be destroyed. Instead, he had his architect Alberti superimpose the Tempio's façade over the old Gothic shell, creating the architectural equivalent of a palimpsest.

The new Renaissance structure was also a translation and a "making new" of Greek architecture, as seen in from this angry report by the prefect of the basilica of S. Apollinaire in Ravenna:

> Filippo, commendatary of the abbazia
> Of Sant Apollinaire, Classe, Cardinal of Bologna
> That he did one night (*quadam nocte*) sell to the
> Illmo D°,D° Sigismund Malatesta
> Lord of Arimininum, marble, porphyry, serpentine,
> Whose men, Sigismundo's, came with more than an hundred
> two wheeled ox carts and deported, for the beautifying
> of the *tempio* where was Santa Maria in Trivio
> Where the same are now on the walls.   (9/36)

In another of his shady contracts, Sigismundo simply bribed Cardinal Filippo of Bologna, "commendatary" of the Abbey of Apollinaire, then quickly sent over some ox carts and hauled off much of the basilica's precious marble to use in the Tempio. Ravenna was outraged by the deal and appealed to Venice, but Malatesta got off with a wrist-slap; a snippet from another document, a "receipt for 200 ducats" paid by Malatesta to the new abbot of S. Apollinaire as "Cornsalve for the damage done in that scurry," testifies to Sigismundo's success in keeping his "translated" marble.

Pound reinforces the image of the Tempio as an architectural channel for the transmission of pagan culture into western Europe by quoting a description of the Tempio from the *Commentaries* of Sigismundo's implacable enemy, Pope Pius II:

> "and built a temple so full of pagan works"
>   i.e. Sigismund
> and in the style "Past ruin'd Latium"
> The filigree hiding the gothic,
>   with a touch of rhetoric in the whole
> And the old sarcophagi,
>   such as lie, smothered in grass, by San Vitale.   (9/41)

Here, at the end of Canto 9, Pound draws together the cultural threads woven into the Tempio—the Renaissance filigree, Gothic understructure, and Byzantine tombs like those at San Vitale. Around these strands Pound interweaves his own textual pillaging of Walter Savage Landor's "Past ruined Ilion Helen lives," linking Isotta, to whom Malatesta dedicated his Tempio, to those other beautiful women like Helen, Eleanor, and Cunizza, who inspire men to create, translate, and transmit beauty. Like them, Isotta is a metamorphosis of Aphrodite, whose temple once stood on the site of the Tempio.

One of the "pagan works" contained in the Tempio is the body of Gemisthus Plethon, a Byzantine Neoplatonist who helped to transmit classical culture to western Europe. In 1438 he attended the Council of Ferrara-Florence as part of the delegation of the "Greek emperor" (8/31), who hoped to unite the eastern and western churches and thus save Constantinople from the Turks. Although the council never forged such an alliance, it brought Plethon to Italy and with him a classical revival. The Neoplatonist's voice, "Talking of the war about the temple at Delphos" and "Telling of how Plato went to Dionysius," inspired Cosimo de Medici to have young Marsilio Ficino tutored in Greek and filled Sigismundo Malatesta with reverence for the pagan world. Plethon's dream of a resurrected Greek empire was never realized, and he died as the Turks were pressing toward Constantinople. But Sigismundo, in his last major military campaign, was sent to fight the invaders in the Peloponnesus; though he failed to stop the Turks, he did bring back Plethon's ashes and place them in one of the Byzantine sarcophagi outside the Tempio.

In another sarcophagus are the ashes of Basinio de Basini, the court poet of Rimini, who once, in a literary tournament presided over by Malatesta, "talked down the anti-Hellene" (9/34), a rival poet who had argued that one need not know the Greek authors in order to write good Latin poetry. Basini demonstrated the essential continuity of Greek and Latin poetry, and Malatesta declared him the winner of the debate. When Malatesta "*templum aedificavit*" ("built a temple"), he also provided a "setting" for the troubadour song "Guillaume Poictiers" brought "up out of Spain" (8/32), thus making the Tempio an "apex" of all the lines of transmission that Pound has traced in these early Cantos.

Malatesta's role as a transmitter of the past is affirmed by another resurrected voice, that of the Renaissance classicist Platina:

> And Platina said afterward,
>   when they jailed him
> And the Accademia Romana,
> For singing to Zeus in the catacombs,
> Yes, I saw him when he was down here
> Ready to murder fatty Barbo, "Formosus,"
> And they want to know what we talked about?
>   "*de litteris et de armis, praestantibusque ingeniis,*
> Both of ancient times and our own; books, arms
> And of men of unusual genius,
> Both of ancient times and our own, in short the usual subjects
> Of conversation between intelligent men."   (11/50-51)

Platina recalls meeting Sigismundo when the condottiere came to Rome ready to kill Pope Paul II for trying to take Rimini from the Malatesta family. The pope, whose real name was Barbo but who wanted to be called "Formosus" ("Handsome") as pope, later arrested humanists like Platina in an effort to stamp out the revival of pagan cults in Rome. Like the earliest Christians, the neopagans worshipped in the catacombs, and the conversation between Platina and Malatesta is part of the underground struggle to preserve the classical past from the historical black-out.

The Church's assault on the new humanism corresponded to its attacks on Malatasta, attacks that finally brought him down and stripped him of his domains. In 1460 Pius II arranged a truce between Sigismundo and other condottieri, but Malatesta broke it by invading the territory of Federigo Urbino. Pius angrily excommunicated Sigismundo and sent an army against him, which Malaesta routed in 1461 at the great battle of Vitelleschi, recounted at the opening of Canto 11. In 1462 Pius burned Malatesta in effigy in Rome and issued an edict—like the edict against the Cid in Canto 3 —forbidding anyone to speak to the Lord of Rimini. The next year Sigismundo was overwhelmed by the combined armies of the pope, Federigo Urbino, and others seeking a piece of the Malatesta domains, and he was forced to accept "de mos' bloody rottenes' peace" (11/49) treaty.

Pound draws his documents from Pius' slanted *Commentaries* as reprinted in Yriarte's appendix: "*Com. Pio II, Liv. VII, p. 85. / Yriarte, p. 288*" (10/44). These ecclesiastical documents black-out Sigismundo in muddy rhetoric that strives for grand flights but only sinks into "bear's-greased latinity" (10/44). Their textual distortion of Malatesta is reflected in Pius' account of the effigy that was ceremonially burned in 1462, an effigy, Pius absurdly claims, that so perfectly resembled Sigismundo that a sign had to be attached to let people know it was not the real thing. Pound solemnly incorporates the ridiculous sign directly into his poem:

> SIGISMUNDO HIC EGO SUM
> MALATESTA, FILIUS PANDULPHI, REX PRODITORUM,
> DEO ATQUE HOMINIBUS INFESTUS, SACRI CENSURA SENATUS
> IGNI DAMNATUS   (10/44)

This sign, in which Malatesta confesses his sins, was stuck in the effigy's mouth, a symbol of the flood of writs that will finally choke Sigismundo in real life.

From the public burning, Pound cuts back to an earlier document in the history of Malatesta's struggles with Pius, the writ of excommunication in 1460—another broken contract—that was read aloud in Rome in 1460 by "that pot-scraping little runt Andreas / Benzi" (10/44), the papal advocate. So overwrought is Benzi's writ that its charges against Malatesta, calling him everything from a rapist to a priest-killer, paint a picture as grossly exaggerated as the supposedly accurate effigy. Some of the charges, in fact, such as practicing the faith of the "epicurae" (10/44), only strengthen Malatesta's role as a conduit for classical culture.

Pound also undercuts Benzi's evidence of a youthful prank that forecast Malatesta's later crimes against the Church:

> And that he did among other things
> Empty the fonts of the chiexa of holy water
> And fill up the same full with ink
> That he might in God's dishonour
> Stand before the doors of the said chiexa
> Making mock of the inky faithful, they
> Issuing thence by the doors in the pale light of the sunrise
> Which might be considered youthful levity
> > but was really a profound indication   (10/44-45)

Pound, too, sees this practical joke as a profound indication of the future, but he reads it as a sign of the Church's decline in the Renaissance, a decline precipitated, in part, by the introduction of printing. The inky fonts transformed by Malatesta reappear in Canto 30 as the new "greek fonts," ironically named after the papal "chancellry letters" (30/148). From these fonts would come the recovered texts of the classical world, a revival of ancient culture which occurred in "Caesar's fane" and coincided with the death of a pope. Hugh Kenner has noted Pound's orthographic pun that follows the announcement "Il Papa mori" with "Explicit canto/XXX"—30 being a printer's sign of cloture. The first text to be inked in these new fonts, furthermore, is "from a codex once of the Lords Malatesta" (30/149).

Pound further counteracts Benzi's indictment by turning his own tropes against him. Benzi's assertion that Malatesta's "foetor" stinks so much it could make "the emparadisèd spirits pewk" (10/45) is undercut by the effigy of Malatesta spewing out the lousy rhetoric of the confessional writ stuffed in its mouth. That rhetoric is itself caught in an excremental metaphor when Pound describes its "whole lump lot" of charges. But that lump lot turns again, this time back against Malatesta, when he enters the Sienese war with Count Pitigliano over worthless land that Broglio describes as "two big lumps of tufa" (9/37). Sigismundo's fundamental troubles were compounded when they "struck alum" (10/46) in the papal territory of "Tolfa," and Pius suddenly had enough money to send an army to drag the condottiere down in the mud.

Pound traces Malatesta's fall through contracts that strip him of his land, followers, and wealth. An oppressive edict drawn up by Pius in 1463 turns over Malatesta's family domains to his enemies:

> *Quali lochi sono questi:*
> Sogliano,
> Torrano and La Serra, Sbrigara, San Martino,
> Ciola, Pondo, Spinello, Cigna and Buchio,
> Prataline, Monte Cogruzzo,
>   and the villa at Rufiano
> Right up to the door-yard
> And anything else the Rev^{mo} Monsignore could remember.
> And the water-rights on the Savio.
> (And the salt heaps with the reed mats on them
>   Gone long ago to the Venetians)
> And when lame Novvy died, they got even Cesena.   (11/49)

Sigismundo's enemies truly "get even" in this usurpation of lands; they even take Cesena with its great library of classical texts, so not only is Malatesta's family domain lost but the cultural heritage he tried to preserve and extend.

As "the writs run in Fano" (11/50), we watch Sigismundo drowning under a swelling tide of documents:

For the long room over the arches
Sub annulo piscatoris, palatium seu curiam OLIM *de Malatestis.*
Gone, and Cesena, Zezena *d'''e b'''e colonne,*
And the big diamond pawned in Venice   (11/50)

Here the contract strips Malatesta of his holdings and places them under the seal of the pope—a seal that shows, appropriately, a fisherman hauling in a big catch. Just one word in the document, "OLIM," quietly enacts the transfer of possessions by stating they were "formerly" held by the Malatestas. The enormous power of the word, of the document, is driven home again by the next pope, Paul II, who forces Malatesta to sign another humiliating contract that further reduces his troops and income:

And he with his luck gone out of him
64 lances in his company, and his pay 8,000 a *year,*
64 and no more, and he not to try to get any more
And all of it down on paper
sexaginta quatuor nec tentatur habere plures   (11/51)

The businesslike "all of it down on paper" shows a Malatesta undone as much by documents as by armies, and the reduction of his group of knights to sixty-four recalls King Lear, who also learned how words could strip one naked.

Still, Pound closes the Malatesta Cantos with a document that resists defeat, a jaunty contract Sigismundo draws up in his final days:

And one day he said: Henry, you can have it,
On condition, you can have it: for four months
You'll stand any reasonable joke that I can play on you,
And you can joke back
        provided you don't get too ornry,
And they put it all down in writing;
for a green cloak with silver brocade
Actum in Castro Sigismundo, presente Roberto de Valturibus
..sponte et ex certa scienta...to Enricho de Aquabello.   (11/52)

The stoic wit with which Malatesta offers his friend the shirt off his back—a shirt that will reappear in the Ugo and Parisina story in Canto 24—cuts against the ecclesiastical documents that have "rendered" the Lord of Rimini. Sigismundo's enduring vitality matches that of the pagan culture he tried to preserve and make new. Pound illustrates that endurance in a letter from the "castelan" (governor) of Montefiore, one of the territories "formerly" in the Malatesta domain, to Pope Paul that warns of the dangerous popularity of Malatesta. "When he got back here from Sparta" (11/51), the governor reports, the citizens greeted him with a torchlight parade; the parade, one of many that will appear in the *Cantos*, is a surviving pagan rite, one that binds together a community. Here, as Malatesta returns from Greece with the ashes of Gemisthus Plethon, the parade indicates that Sigismundo and the classical world he transmitted have survived the historical black-out: "In the gloom, the gold gathers the light against it" (11/51).

III

The Printing House of Hell

By the twentieth century, the mud that dragged down Malatesta—the "alum at Tolfa," the "lumps of tufa," the "lump lot of his enemies," and all the other "pius crap"—engulfs the whole world in the excremental waste of usury, a "blacker and rich mud," a "new dung-flow," the "petrification of putrefaction" (15/64). In the "Hell Cantos" (14 through 16) Pound compounds scatalogy and eschatology to paint an infernal printing house that covers the modern world in "sh-t":

> howling, as of a hen-yard in a printing-house,
>   the clatter of presses,
> the blowing of dry dust and stray paper,
> foetor, sweat, the stench of stale oranges,
> dung, last cess-pool of the universe,
> mysterium, acid of sulphur,
> the pusillanimous, raging;
> plunging jewels in mud,
> . . . .
> black-beetles, burrowing into the sh-t,
> The soil a decrepitude, the ooze full of morsels,
> lost contours, erosions.   (14/61-62)

While infernal metaphors for printing are common enough—we speak of "printer's devils," for instance—Pound may have in mind the "Printing House in Hell" in Blake's The Marriage of Heaven and Hell, particularly since he alludes to Blake in Canto 16 at the close of his journey through hell.[1]

In The Marriage of Heaven and Hell the "Printing House" of hell is Blake's own print shop, where he produces illuminated texts "by printing in the infernal method by corrosives, which in hell are salutary and medicinal, melting apparent surfaces away, and displaying the infinite which was hid."[2] Thus, Blake reverses traditional notions of hell to celebrate his "infernal" method of printing, which purges, cleanses, and heals—processes that reflect his practice of etching his plates with acid. Such a process, as Clark Emery notes, "supplants machined black type with characterful script, makes white paper joyfully colorful, brings to the eye the naked human form divine, and, in sum, opens up the chinks of man's cavern using the corrosive acid of satire and burlesque."[3] Blake's purgatorial acid cleanses the rhetoric, the dogma, the lies churned out by society's printing presses to foster the official version of heaven—which Blake depicts as a hellish pit full of squabbling, dung-eating monkeys.

Pound develops a similar opposition by portraying hell as a vast printing house that excretes propaganda for the religious, political, and financial establishment. Hell is filled with ink-bespattered sheets of paper: "british weeklies" (15/65) and "Flies carrying news" (14/63). The daily newspaper, the "dirt sheet," is a perfect instance of the economics of waste because it is designed to be consumed and then thrown away—the antithesis of the documents Pound treasured. The "press gang" copulates with the usurers and munitions-makers in Pound's hell, for all symbolically feast on excrement by making their living from the production and distribution of waste products. In Canto 18 we witness an apt instance of this filthy union in the "press gang" whose newspapers laud the arms-maker Metevsky as "the well-known philan-thropist" (18/81). A few lines earlier we saw how the wasteful destruction of an expensive weapon—a torpedo boat whose instrument panel is described, significantly, as "about like the size ov / A typewriter"—leads to profitable new orders.

The wastefulness of arms-makers and newspapers is complemented by the publications of the academy, and we should not be surprised to learn that a financier like Metevsky shrewdly endows universities. Pound describes a hell of constipated scholars "sitting on piles of stone books, / obscuring the texts with philology" and equates them with "monopolists, obstructors of knowledge, / obstructors of distribution" (14/63). Meanwhile, truly worthwhile and durable texts are suppressed and kept out of print. Douglas's work on Social Credit is rejected for publication by another economist, who fears "it would make my own seem so out of date" (22/102). Similarly, Pound's proposed anthology of enduring poems is turned down by "MacNarpen and Company," who are afraid it might rival their big moneymaker, "Palgrave's Golden Treasury" (22/102). Yet, even as these valuable texts are suppressed, the printing-house of hell churns on, grinding out the utterly useless deluge of "200 copies" of "Floradora in sheets" (27/130).

Another suppression of vital documents opens Canto 19:

> Sabotage? Yes, he took it up to Manhattan,
> To the big company, and they said: Impossible.

And he said: I gawt ten thousand dollars tew mak 'em,
And I am a goin' tew mak 'em, and you'll damn well
Have to install 'em, awl over the place.
And they said: Oh, we can't have it.
So he settled for one-half of one million.
And he has a very nice place on the Hudson,
And that invention, patent, is still in their desk.   (19/84)

Here the suppression of the patent for the telephone, an instrument designed to carry the human voice, is related to the conflict Pound saw between speech and print in modern world. As Max Nänny has shown, Pound's love of the spoken word led to a "growing revulsion against most manifestations of literacy, hating bookishness and book-culture, distrusting the written and printed words, and loathing the very act of reading."[4]

When the Chinese invention of block printing was adapted in medieval Europe, it promised to disseminate ancient documents and generate a cultural renewal. By the twentieth century, however, printing, according to Pound, had become "a midden, a filth, a mere smear" that equals any "mediaeval description of hell."[5] Through the corrosive acid of processes like Blake's engraving, Pound suggests that the printed text must be grounded again in what Nänny calls the "true shaping force behind Pound's poetry and prose"—"the mould of talk."[6] We see such a purgatorial cleansing in Canto 12 where Pound's friend John Quinn drawls out in thick dialect his "pore honest sailor" joke at a banker's meeting. This bit of oral folklore pours a crude but cleansing acid over the hypocrisy and pomposity of the "ranked presbyterians" and equates their usurious profits with the unnatural products of sodomy.

The same purgatorial acid of satire enables Pound the pilgrim to escape from the printing house of hell:

And before hell mouth; dry plain
        and two mountains;
On the one mountain, a running form,
        and another
In the turn of the hill; in hard steel
The road like a slow screw's thread,
The angle almost imperceptible,
        so that the circuit seemed hardly to rise;
And the running form, naked, Blake,
Shouting, whirling his arms, the swift limbs,
Howling against the evil,
        his eyes rolling,
Whirling like flaming cart-wheels,
        and his head held backward to gaze on the evil
As he ran from it,
        to be hid by the steel mountain   (16/68)

Pound's vision is illustrated by one of the engravings for the deluxe edition of *A Draft of XVI Cantos* printed in Paris in 1925. He was especially pleased with this edition, handsomely printed with drawings and ornate capital letters, for it resembled a medieval illuminated manuscript. The engraving for Canto 16 shows a Blake-like figure ascending a purgatorial mountain, and Pound's description emphasizes the technique of Blake's printing as an antidote for the products of hell's printing presses. The very acid that Blake used to etch his words and figures becomes a purgatorial fire: the criminals are caught "lying in blue lakes of acid" as Blake's satire exposes the rhetoric of the official press, and Pound's pilgrim emerging from "hell-mouth" bathes "with the acid" to rid himself of "the hell ticks" before he ascends the "steel mountain" of the engraving plate.

Through such corrosive satire as John Quinn's folk tales and Blake's acid plates, Pound's pilgrim ascends to the top of the purgatorial mountain and lies down in a paradise filled with human voices:

> The plain, distance, and in fount-pools
>   the nymphs of that water
> rising, spreading their garlands,
>   weaving their water reeds with the boughs,
> In the quiet,
>   and now one man rose from his fountain
> and went off into the plain.
>
> Prone in that grass, in sleep;
>   et j'entendis des voix:...   (16/69-70)

The shift to French emphasizes the oral quality of this paradise where human voices rise from the print on the page, talking with clarity and grace that transcend the "howling" of hell: Victor Plarr reliving his boyhood memories of Galliffet's charge in the Franco-Prussian War, Admiral Percy's anecdote of Lord Byron, delivered in a voice that "pulled it out long, like that: / the face of an a y n . . . . gel"; Pound's own voice slangily recounting stories of World War I that he heard from the mouths of T.E. Hulme and Ernest Hemingway, and Fernand Léger doing the same in a demotic French that asserts its spoken nature with "Poo quah" and "O voui"; and, finally, Lincoln Steffens lecturing on the Russian Revolution and mimicking the shifting and contending voices of soldiers and citizens that erupt over a quietly spoken "Pojalouista" (16/75). While these are the voices of paradise, their subject is not heaven but the hell of war, and what they say of it purges the lies propagated by the printing house of hell.

This paradise of voices, in turn, echoes the conversation of Kung (Confucius) and his disciples in a cedar grove in Canto 13. Pound sees in Kung a figure bent upon the same task he himself has undertaken in *The Cantos*—the preserving, compiling, and making new of the vital documents of the past. "I transmit and do not create," Kung said, believing, like Pound, that the only way to combat the turmoil and corruption of his age was to renew the documents of the past.[7] Even as he preserved these documents, Kung realized that the written texts emerged from the spoken word. *The Analects*, records written by Kung's disciples of their conversations with the master, stress Kung's role as a source of "the oral tradition,"[8] and Pound tried to reflect their conversational character when he translated them, not from the original but from a French translation:

> And Kung said
> > "You old fool, come out of it,
> Get up and do something useful."   (13/59)

Pound's tries to capture the natural sound of Kung's voice in a written text, much as Kung himself did when he "wrote on the bo leaves."

Like Kung's disciples, who reverently preserved these organic texts, Pound describes himself as a translator and retransmitter of delicate documents:

> The blossoms of the apricot
> > blow from the east to the west,
> And I have tried to keep them from falling.   (13/60)

The blossoms from the apricot grove where Kung lectured are, like the bo leaves, texts that Pound is trying to transplant carefully enough to preserve their oral grace and power. His translation of the *Analects*, as one critic has remarked, constitutes an "essential document in the history of Oriental-Western literary relations."[9]

Kung's bo leaves are metamorphosed again in Canto 18, where Pound takes a leaf from Marco Polo's *Il Milione*:

> "I have told you of that emperor's city in detail
> And will tell you of the coining in Cambaluc
> > that hyght the secret of alchemy:
> They take bast of the mulberry-tree,
> That is a skin between the wood and the bark,
> And of this they make paper, and mark it
> Half a tornesel, a tornesel, or a half-groat of silver,
> Or two groats, or five groats, or ten groats,
> Or, for a great sheet, a gold bezant, 3 bezants,
> > ten bezants;
> And they are written on by officials,
> And smeared with the great khan's seal in vermilion   (18/80)

Like other documents as in *The Cantos*, the record of Marco Polo's journey opened a vital channel between cultures. He composed *Il Milione* in 1296 while he was in prison at Genoa during its trade wars with Venice—an eerie foreshadowing of Pound's own imprisonment in Pisa. In light of Pound's stress on oral documents, it is significant that Marco Polo dictated his memoirs to a French writer who was also in prison. In the excerpt Pound adapts, Polo transmits vital news of Kublai Khan's paradise on earth, not a poetic dream-world but a heavenly city grounded on such prosaic alchemy as economic regulation. The currency issued by Kublai is the financial metamorphosis of Kung's bo leaves—money rooted in the organic wealth of the land and distributed carefully over the earth by a wise and generous ruler. Bo leaves, apricot blossoms, and the leaves of Blake's illuminated books all render the human voice and thus offset, appropriately, the filthy sheets of the printing house of hell.

IV

Civic Accounts

In Cantos XVII-XXX Pound drew upon the great documentary treasures of Italian archives to perform his own alchemy—transforming dry municipal records into visions of splendid Renaissance cities. The mystical evocation of Venice that opens Canto 17, rising from the sea at dawn, is balanced in Canto 25 by prosaic documents tracing the bureaucratic squabbles that attended the building of the Palace of the Doges. Pound drew upon a collection of documents about the palace compiled by Giambattista Lorenzi in *Monumenti per servire alla storia del Palazzo Ducale di Venezia*. In gathering these records Lorenzi was following the advice of John Ruskin, who in *The Stones of Venice* said that to understand the architecture of the palace, one had to study the documents that trace its construction and remodeling from the late thirteenth century to the mid-1500s.[1] In recasting Lorenzi's catalogue, Pound counterpoints the beauty of the palace, a metamorphosis of Aphrodite in stone, with the ruthless Venetian Council that pushed remodeling of the palace to satisfy its growing sense of self-importance.

Like Malatesta's Tempio, the Palace of the Doges is an architectural palimpsest whose layers of Byzantine, Gothic, and Renaissance styles reflect the centuries of construction and remodeling detailed in the council records. Pound picks up the story where Lorenzi does, with the "BOOK OF THE COUNCIL MAJOR" (25/115) in the late thirteenth century, where the Great Council grumbles about its cramped quarters on the ground floor of the old palace:

> 1255 be it enacted:
> That they mustn't shoot crap in the hall
> of the council, nor in the small court under
> pain of 20 danari, be it enacted:
> 1266 no squire of Venice to throw dice
> *anywhere* in the palace or
> in the loggia of the Rialto under pain of ten soldi

> or half that for kids, and if they wont pay
> they are to be chucked in the water. (25/115)

This "curious document," according to historian Terisio Pignatti, marks the beginning of the modifications that would transfigure the palace, a transformation that paralleled the growth of the council's power.[2]

In the next entry, from 1316, the palace has been modified. Beneath the new quarters provided for the council by Doge Soranzo, we witness the mating of two caged lions and the subsequent birth, on St. Mark's Day, of "three lion cubs":

> living and hairy which born at once began life and motion
> and to go gyring about their mother throughout the
> aforesaid room as saw the aforesaid Lord Doge and as it
> were all the Venetians and other folk who were in
> Venice that day that concurred all for this as it were
> miraculous sight. And one of the animals is a male
> and the other two female
>   I John Marchesini Ducal notary of the
>   Venetians as eyewitness saw the
>   nativity of these animals thus by
>   mandate of the said Doge wrote this
>   and put it in file. (25/116)

Through this solemn, bureaucratic entry—in the register for foreign affairs, no less—we can see voyeuristic counselors gazing at their caged beasts. Soon they are paying "the procurators of St. Mark" for lions of gilt and stone to adorn their swelling palace.

That palace, however, continues to be a prison, and in 1327 the council passes a grim ordinance allowing the exiled daughter of Doge Soranzo to return to the city to nurse her dying father:

> Be it enacted:
> to Donna Sorantia Soranzo that she come for the
> feast of the Ascension by night in a covered boat and
> alight at the ripa del Palazzo, and when first sees the
> Christblood go at once up into the Palace and may
> stay in the Palace VIII days to visit the Doge her
> father not in that time leaving the palace, nor
> descending the palace stair and when she descends it
> that she return by night the boat in the like manner
> being covered. To be revoked at the council's pleasure.
>   accepted by 5 of the council (25/116-17)

Like the caged lions, the young girl remained in the palace, as a nun, for the rest of her life. Soon the gorgeous palazzo begins to "stink" from its "dungeons" full of prisoners, and that stench (25/117) prompts the council to make more extensive modifications.

The key document in that architectural metamorphosis was the 1340 plan submitted by a subcommittee of Three Elders, "Marc Erizio, / Nic. Speranzo, Tomasso Gradonico" (25/117), which overhauled the palace to build for the council a magnificent hall overlooking the Grand Canal. By Pound's arrangement of these records, the expanding council seems to be crowding out the doge both literally and figuratively—he "can scarce / stand upright in his bedroom" (25/117) and is becoming a mere figurehead in Venetian politics. The sumptuous remodeling called for in the plan of the Three Elders became so expensive that construction had to be halted and could not even be discussed again until the early fifteenth century, when the doge's complaints about the relative meagerness of his quarters renewed the issue and led to a historic vote, which Pound records, to execute the plan of the Three Elders.

From these bare documents Pound cuts to a lyrical evocation of the palace itself:

> Which is to say: they built out over the arches
> and the palace hangs there in the dawn, the mist,
> in that dimness,
> or as one rows in from past the murazzi
> the barge slow after moon-rise
> and the voice sounding under the sail.   (25/117)

The shift from documentary to lyrical textures here parallels the contrast between the beauty of the Palace of the Doges and the seamy politics of the council that erected it. The same contrast colors Pound's shift back to the documentary mode at the end of Canto 25, to trace the contractual squabbles between the council and Titian over a mural for the Hall of the Council. In Titian the council meets an artist with its own mercantile temperament, as we see in his initial bid:

> ...side toward the piazza, the worst side of the room
> that no one has been willing to tackle,
> and do it as cheap or much cheaper...
>   (signed) Tician, 31 May 1513   (25/119)

Titian's commercial pitch here marks the decay of the arts as surely as does his painting, in which Pound saw a falling off from the clarity of early Renaissance art, which eventually led to the "raw meat" of Rubens and the "brown meat" of Rembrandt (80/511).

Titian's bid is followed by a council decree of 1522 threatening the painter with the loss of the lucrative brokerage he had been promised if he does not complete the painting. The fact that Titian not only wants a seat on the stock exchange but that the one he gets had been held by Bellini underscores the mutual corruption of art and economics under usury, facts Pound will hammer home in the famous "Usury Canto":

> With *Usura*
>
> With usura hath no man a house of good stone
> each block cut smooth and well fitting
> that design might cover their face,
> with usura
> hath no man a painted paradise on his church wall   (45/229)

In the final document of Canto 25, the Venetian Senate votes overwhelmingly to strip Titian of his house and profits:

> the said profits WHEREFORE
>   be it moved that the said
> Tician de Cadore, pictor, be by authority of this Council
> obliged and constrained to restore to our government all the
> moneys that he has had from the agency during the time he
> has not worked on the painting in the said
> hall as is reasonable
>   ayes 102, noes 38, 37 undecided
>   register of the senate
>   terra 1537, carta 136.   (25/120)

Here in 1537, nearly twenty-five years after the original contract was made, Titian loses his brokerage house and the council still does not have its mural.

Pound follows the decay of politics and art in Venice in Canto 26, but he moves away from Lorenzi's documents to a wide range of commercial, military, and diplomatic texts that he found in the Venetian archives and in such collections as Muratori's twenty-six volume *Rerum Italicarum Scriptores*. The Canto opens in twentieth-century Venice, with Pound himself in his "young youth" (26/121), lying like a prisoner "under the crocodile" statue—penniless, exiled from a world that has no use for his art, his only prospects the succession of views from the sides of St. Mark's Square. His plight takes him back to Renaissance Venice and a document that records the imprisonment of another artist, Matteo di Pasti:

> "Relaxetur!"
> 11th. December 1461: that Pasti be let out
>   with a caveat

"caveat ire ad Turchum, that he stay out of
          Constantinople
"if he hold dear our government's pleasure.
"The book will be retained by the council
          (the book being Valturio's "Re Militari").   (26/121)

Here the council releases the artist but suppresses the document he was
carrying—Roberto Valturio's *De Re Militaria*, a book about military explosives
and fortifications for which Pasti had done the designs. Sigismundo Malatesta
had commissioned Pasti to do a portrait of Mohammed II, the Turkish
emperor, and had sent along Valturio's book as a present. Though Pound
presents this document as another instance of the oppressiveness of the
Venetian government, he confirms the council's suspicion that Malatesta's
explosive gift is designed to create an alliance between Rimini and the Turks.

Those shifting suspicions and alliances surface again in Venetian diplomatic
documents that present a new slant on the crushing defeat that Malatesta
suffered in his war with Pope Pius II. The Venetian Senate, in dispatches to
"Nicolo Segundino," its ambassador to Rome, strikes a peace-making role
between the warring sides; however, Pound's handling of the document,
"Faithful sons (we are) of the church / (for two pages)…" (26/121), shows that
the public stance is a hypocritical cover-up to keep the war going. Another
document, recording the senate's dealings with Malatesta's envoy, "Messire
Hanibal," further reveals Venetian duplicity:

Senato Secreto, 28th of October,
Came Messire Hanibal from Cesena:
"Cd. they hoist the flag of St. Mark
"And have Fortinbras and our army?"
"They cd. not…but on the quiet, secretissime,
"Two grand…Sic : He may have
"Two thousand ducats; himself to hire the men
"From our army."   (26/122)

Pound lets these secret minutes unravel the senate's cloak of neutrality: while
they publicly refuse to allow Malatesta's forces to fly the Venetian flag, they
slip Hanibal "Two grand" under the table for the purpose of hiring soldiers from
the Venetian army along with one of their own commanders, a condottiere
named, significantly, Fortinbras. As the war depletes other Italian cities,
Venice grows fat—a point which Pound makes with snippets of trade records
that testify to Venetian monopoly of trade from England to the Levant.

Pound then turns back to documents from an earlier period in Venetian
history, before the rise of the oligarchy, when Venice was ruled by powerful
doges. He organizes these records around three public festivals celebrating the

coronations of doges Selvo (in 1071), Lorenzo Tiepolo (1268), and Tommaso Mocenigo (1414). Although Selvo's Byzantine wife Theodora is castigated by chroniclers for the "luxuria" of eating with golden forks, the doge bestows a far greater opulence on the city by putting up mosaics in the basilica, thus beginning the process of artistic transfiguration that would culminate in the Palace of the Doges.

The coronation of another doge, Lorenzo Tiepolo, is marked by a parade of tradesmen in elaborate costumes that symbolize their guilds:

> Barbers, heads covered with beads,
> Furriers, masters in rough,
> Master pelters for fine work,
> And the masters for lambskin
> With silver cups and their wine flasks
> And blacksmiths with the gonfaron
>   et leurs fioles chargies de vin,
> The masters of wool cloth
> Glass makers in scarlet
> Carrying fabrefactions of glass   (26/122)

Once again in *The Cantos* the communal rite of a parade celebrates a city organized by guilds and ruled by a doge who regulates civic life and stimulates the arts—a vision of the Italy Pound believed was emerging under Mussolini.

The third festival, the coronation of Doge Mocenigo in April of 1414, symbolizes a falling away from that ideal. The festivities are marked by conspicuous consumption and the kind of exorbitant fees and spectacular entertainment one finds nowadays at a big state fair: "it cost three ducats to rent any horse" in the medieval equivalent of a demolition derby—a joust with "three hundred and fifty horses" and "In the last fight fourteen on a side"(26/123). To this festival come Niccolò d'Este of Ferrara and Francesco Gonzaga of Mantua, and they reappear in 1438, in another parade, on their way to the Council of Ferrara-Florence. This great East-West ecclesiastical convention, glimpsed earlier in the Malatesta Cantos, is here seen through an eyewitness account by a Venetian man-on-the-street who watches the entourage from Constantinople and guffaws, "you would have bust your bum laughing / To see the hats and beards of those greeks" (26/124). The presence of "Cosimo Medici" and "Lord Sigismundo da Rimini" in the parade, however, foreshadows the revival of Greek culture in Italy.

That revival is sparked by the key figure in the Greek emperor's contingent, "Gemisto" Plethon, the great Neoplatonist who debated the Nicene Creed with a Roman ecclesiastic:

And in February they all packed off
To Ferrara to decide on the holy ghost
And as to the which beget the what in the Trinity.—
Gemisto and the Stonolifex   (26/123)

Plethon's victory centered upon a document—an appendix to the Nicene Creed that the Western Church used to support its claim that the Holy Ghost emanated from both the Father and the Son. By revealing the document to be a forgery, Plethon justified the position of the Eastern Church that the Holy Ghost came from the Father alone. Plethon, as we have seen, was not interested in the niceties of Christian theology but in the renewal of pagan culture, and, while he never got his Greek empire in the Peloponnesus, his conversations did inspire Cosimo and Sigismundo with a reverence for classical culture.

Even as these figures wind through Venice, the city's "guild spirit" is declining, and the oligarchy has reduced the doge to a mere master of ceremonies who annually weds Aphrodite by casting a gold ring into the sea. The senate, by contrast, shrewdly dispenses silk and silver to condottieri like Carlo and Pandolfo Malatesta to keep them "in mood to go on with the fighting" (26/124) in Venetian wars. Similarly, it bestows an ambassadorship on the exiled Cosimo de Medici, who was soon to regain control of Florence, and an estate to another condottiere, "Lord Luigi Gonzaga," whose family would soon take over Mantua. By inserting an ordinance regulating prostitutes—the "young ladies" who are required to wear a "yellow kerchief"—Pound makes a silent comment on Venice's procurement of military and diplomatic favors.

The height of Venetian treachery came at the Fall of Constantinople, when the council ignored pleas from "the church of the orient"; from Sigismundo Malatesta, who "left Mantua" after urging a vigorous defense of the Peloponnesus; and from the Byzantine emperor, who desperately begged for Venetian aid. After the collapse of the city, Venice struck a cynical trade agreement with the victorious Moslems:

> "Venetians may stand, come, depart with their families
> Free by land, free by sea
>   in their galleys,
> Ships, boats, and with merchandise.
> 2% on what's actually sold. No tax above that.
>   Year 6962 of the world
>   18th. April, in Constantinople."
> Wind on the lagoon, the south wind breaking roses.   (26/125)

The closing image of "breaking wind" connects the stench of the lagoons with the usurious war profiteering of Venice to give us a whiff of what by the twentieth century will be the universal fetor of hell.

Once again, usury spills over into art, and Pound makes his documentary point with letters from three oppressed artists: Pisanellus begging his patron, Count Sforza, to be allowed "to take myself out of" Bologna (26/125), where Sforza had sent him to buy horses; "Victor Carpathio" (26/127) pleading with Francesco Gonzaga for payment for a painting taken by one of Gonzaga's agents; and Mozart, writing to "the supreme pig, the archbishop of Salzburg" (26/128), demanding to be allowed to leave the city. The fact that Pisanellus must flatter and cajole Sforza to be released from Bologna is bad enough, but Carpathio's groveling to Gonzaga is a nauseating indication of how an artist must debase himself as a "humble svt. of yr. Sublimity" (26/127). The actual letter from Mozart to the Archbishop of Salzburg is written in the same humble tones, but Pound vengefully reads between the lines ("*inter lineas*") to imagine Mozart's real feelings for his patron.[3] The latent invective that Pound extracts from this letter is then set against the delicacy of feeling evident in another letter Mozart writes, to his father, comparing his new sonata to the beauty of his pupil, Rosa Cannabich, who is another metamorphosis of Aphrodite struggling for expression in a usurious age.

The fact that Mozart's oppressive patron is the archbishop helps Pound document another aspect of the breakdown of culture in the Renaissance—the end of the Church's role as patron of the arts. The gaudy silver-plating of "the head of St. George the Martyr" (26/126) shows the Church wallowing in the very usury it once outlawed. A letter from the Spanish ambassador to Venice, Diego "Mendoça" (26/126), implicates Cardinal Gonzaga of Mantua in the plot to assassinate Lorenzo Medici, who, as Pound recounted in Canto 5, had killed his cousin Alesandro. Because Alesandro had been married to the daughter of the Holy Roman Emperor Charles V of Spain, the Spanish court avenged the murder by having Lorenzo killed in Venice. In this document, the Spanish ambassador instructs the cardinal to help in protecting the assassins by circulating false reports of their whereabouts. For Pound, this seamy murder was just one more sign of the collapse of Renaissance promise.

Before that collapse, however, the classical renewal had taken hold in Ferrara under the rule of Niccolò d'Este, a shrewd diplomat who preserved his city from larger neighbors like Venice. Pound emphasizes the Este family's importance as a channel for the transmission of the classical world by alluding to the myth that the dynasty descended from Trojan refugees who had landed on the Italian coast, "cut holes in rock," "put up the timbers," and "condit Atesten" (20/90-91). Niccolò, a reincarnation of Odysseus, made a voyage to Greece and the Holy Land in 1413:

And he in his young youth, in the wake of Odysseus
To Cithera (a. d. 1413) "dove fu Elena rapta da Paris"
Dinners in orange groves, prows attended of dolphins,
Vestige of Rome at Pola, fair wind as far as Naxos
Ora vela, ora a remi, sino ad ora di vespero
Or with the sail tight hauled, by the crook'd land's arm
Zefalonia
And at Corfu, greek singers; by Rhodos
Of the windmills, and to Paphos,
Donkey boys, dust, deserts, Jerusalem, backsheesh
And an endless fuss over passports;
One groat for the Jordan, whether you go there or not,
The school where the madonna in girlhood
Went to learn letters   (24/111)

The contrast between rapturous singing amid lush orange groves and a dusty tourist trap of bureaucratic tangles underscores for Pound the difference between pagan vitality and a Hebraic-Christian wasteland.

Niccolò's youthful odyssey converted him to Hellenism and inspired him to found the great library of Ferrara and fill it with classical texts and translations. It was in that vast archive that the document recording Niccolò's voyage, an eyewitness account written by his Latin secretary, Luchino dal Campo, was accidentally discovered. As with Malatesta's Sienese post-bag, dal Campo's *Viaggio a Gerusalemme di Niccolò da Este* turned up among some old papers, and the scholar who found and published the document celebrated dal Campo's prose as the embodiment of the fresh Tuscan speech of the Renaissance.[4] In one of those fresh phrases, "dove fu Elena rapta da Paris" (where Helen was raped by Paris), however, Pound reads a grimmer way in which Niccolò renewed the classical past.

Like Menelaus, Niccolò learned that his young wife, Parisina Malatesta, was having an affair with his bastard son, Ugo, so he had the young lovers executed. Working through documents in "the book of the mandates" (24/110), the *Registro Mandati* of the Este family, Pound retells the pathetic tale of young lovers and old cuckold.

Thus the book of the mandates:
              Feb. 1422.
We desire that you our factors give to Zohanne of
        Rimini
our servant, six lire marchesini,
for the three prizes he has won racing our barbarisci,
at the rate we have agreed on. The races he has won
are the Modena, the San Petronio at Bologna
and the last race at San Zorzo.
        (Signed) Parisina Marchesa   (24/110)

This first entry from the *Registro* is Parisina's authorization of payments to her jockey, "Zohanne of Rimini," for winning races with her barbary, and through it we glimpse a young bride as restive as one of her own horses.

The mention of Rimini establishes a parallel between Parisina and Dante's Francesca, and the next entry reinforces the analogy, as Parisina authorizes payment for "binding / un libro franxese che si chiama Tristano" (24/110). This French romance about the adulterous love of Tristan and Iseult rhymes with the book that served as a pimp, a "galeotto," for Paolo and Frances- ca—the tale of Lancelot and Guinevere. Through this textual overlap, Pound suggests that both affairs are inspired not so much by passion but by the imitation of desire recorded in a book. The image of Niccolò in later years, entangled in a jungle of artifice figured in the bewildering arras on his palace wall, extends the parallel with Dante's literary lovers, for Paolo, too, was trapped in an arras and killed as he tried to escape from Francesca's husband—an image not only of literal entanglement but of the bewildering confusion of life and art that infects the Ferrara of the Estes.

Snippets from other entries in the register show Parisina buying frills, "perfumes, parrot seeds, combs"; reining in her spendthrift jockey; and splurging "25 ducats" on a green tunic, a "ziparello," for her stepson Ugo. This is the same green cloak that Sigismundo wagered against "Enricho de Aquabello" (11/52), and it reminds us that Parisina was a Malatesta, one of the "tribe" that "paid always" (8/32). The cloak also suggests the eventual degeneration of Ferrara into a "paradiso dei sarti" (24/114), a paradise for clothiers, and Pound reinforces the suggestion by playing off Parisina's "predeletto" (24/110), her preference for a green cloak for Ugo, to the "per diletto" of the Ferrarese aesthetes "that read all day" and leave "the night work to the servants" (24/114).[5]

Such aesthetic escapism is as damning to art as Venetian usury, and in Canto 20 Pound locates the same sins in his own age and in himself. As in *Hugh Selwyn Mauberley*, he exorcises his own temptation to pursue sirens' songs —Homer's "Ligur' aoide" (20/89) and Arnaut Daniel's "*e l'olors— / ...d'enoi ganres*" (20/90)—into a lotus-land of aesthetic escapism whose heady "smell banishes sadness."[6] During a literary odyssey in his own "young youth," Pound had copied some of Daniel's honeyed lines from a manuscript in the aptly named "Ambrosiana" Library and had taken them to "old Lévy" (20/89), the Provençal scholar who, like Tiresias, devours the young questor's offering and then asks, "Now is there anything I can tell you?" (20/89).

In Canto 24, however, Pound steers clear of the sirens' song of lyrical indulgence by staying with documents whose prosaic texture, far from banishing sadness, underscore it with such flat entries as the dowry Niccolò's second son, Leonello Este, arranges for his sister:

(27 nov. 1427)
PROCURATIO NOMINE PATRIS, Leonello Este
(arranging dot for Margarita his sister, to
Roberto Malatesta of Rimini)
natae praelibati margaritae
Ill. D. Nicolai Marchionis Esten. et Sponsae:
The tower of Gualdo
with plenary jurisdiction in civils; and in criminal:
to fine and have scourged all delinquents
as in the rest of their lands,
"which things
this tower, estate at Gualdo had the Illustrious
Nicolaus Marquis of Este received from the said
Don Carlo (Malatesta)
for dower
Illustrae Dominae Parisinae Marxesana."

> under my hand D. Michaeli de Magnabucis
> Not. pub. Ferr.
> D. Nicolaeque Guiduccioli de Arimino.
> Sequit bonorum descriptio.   (24/110-11)

The bureaucratic texture of this contract, which Pound reproduces down to
the notary public's signature, clashes with the tragedy that spawns it. In the
time between Parisina's entry for a green cloak for Ugo and this document, the
two lovers have been executed, yet all we witness is the crisp efficiency of
Leonello in his role as "procurator," soothing Parisina's relatives by arranging
another marriage between the Estes and Malatestas, and returning to Rimini
the Malatesta holdings that had been part of Parisina's dowry when she married
Niccolò.

At this point Pound interjects dal Campo's record of Niccolò's voyage to
Greece and the Holy Land, a documentary flashback that contrasts the
vigorous youth with the bitter cuckold. Returning to the present, we find the
documentary record of the executions:

> Was beheaded Aldovrandino (1425, vent'uno Maggio)
> Who was cause of this evil, and after
> The Marchese asked was Ugo beheaded. And the Captain
> "Signor...si." and il Marchese began crying
> "Fa me hora tagliar la testa
> "dapoi cosi presto hai decapitato il mio Ugo."
> Rodendo con denti una bachetta che havea in mani.
> And passed that night weeping, and calling Ugo, his son.   (24/112)

Pacing the halls all night with a sword in his teeth, Niccolò begs his guards to cut off his head as they did Ugo's. For his wife and all women, however, he has only bitterness, and he not only executes Parisina's friend Aldovrandino, the go-between in the affair, but issues a writ punishing all adultresses with decapitation, "That his should not suffer alone" (24/113).

Pound wryly notes that Niccolò "in '31 married Monna Ricarda" and then cuts abruptly to another document, a grant of a French coat of arms to the Este family from Charles VII of France. The date and place of the grant create an ironic documentary rhyme between Parisina and Joan of Arc, who was tried at Chinon and burned in 1431. Such juxtapositions undercut Niccolò's posture of moral avenger, as does Pound's characterization of him as the leader who "brought seduction in place of / Rape into government" (24/112). Similarly, in the elaborate funeral festivities that Niccolò arranged for Ugo there was a three-hundred gun salute, which Pound describes as a "Tre cento 'bastardi' (or bombardi fired off at his funeral)" to suggest the many "bastardi" Niccolò was said to have fathered.

After quickly noting the events of Niccolò's last years—the birth of his son Ercole and the loss of Ravenna by the Polenta family, a loss that prefigured the eventual takeover of Ferrara by its ravenous neighbor, Venice—Pound quotes from Niccolò's testament where he modestly asks to be buried "without decoration" (24/113). The Canto ends with a conversation between Pound and an Italian librarian:

> And if you want to know what became of his statue,
> I had a rifle class in Bondeno
> And the priest sent a boy to the hardware
> And he brought back the nails in a wrapping,
> And it was the leaf of a diary
> And he got the rest from the hardware
>   (Cassini, libraio, speaking)
> And on the first leaf of the wrapping
> Was how in Napoleon's time
> Came down a load of brass fittings from Modena
> Via del Po, all went by the river,
> To Piacenza for cannon, bells, door-knobs
> And the statues of the Marchese Niccolò and of Borso
> That were in the Piazza on columns.
> And the Commendatore has made it a monograph
> Without saying I told him and sent him
> The name of the priest.   (24/113-14)

This refreshing voice recounts another of the many documentary finds in *The Cantos*—the fragments of a nineteenth-century diary that records the fate of Niccolò's and Borso's statues. Just as the melting down of those statues into cannons marks the failure of the Estes to "keep the peace," so the diary is being used to wrap military hardware. It is a military man, too, the local "Commendatore," who confiscates and publishes the text without giving credit to the priest and the librarian who recovered the lost document. Niccolò's failure to establish an enduring cultural center in Ferrara is further shown by the sale of his magnificent Schifanoia palace to a "tanning" factory (24/114). The murals in that palace, by Cosimo de Tura, are "Painted to look like arras" (20/91) in an aesthetic mirroring of artifice upon artifice that leaves the aged Niccolò delirious in an aesthetic "Wilderness of renewals, confusion" (20/92). "After him and his day," we learn, all of Ferrara turned into a lotus-land of "cake-eaters" and "consumers of icing" (24/114).[7]

Just as Venice is rendered through its council records and Ferrara through the *Registro Mandati*, Florence is presented through an equally appropriate set of documents—the account books of the Medici family. In Canto 21 Pound conjures the image of Lorenzo de Medici poring over "Cosimo's red leather note book" and his own "big green account book" (21/96), just as Pound himself goes over these documents centuries later in the Laurenziana archives. Through these textual layers voice calls to voice, Lorenzo resurrecting Cosimo's dead voice from the family accounts. Cosimo, in turn, transmits the dying words of his father, Giovanni:

> "Keep on with the business,
>   That's made me,
> "And the res publica didn't.
> "When I was broke, and a poor kid,
> "They all knew me, all of these *cittadini*,
> "And they all of them cut me dead, della gloria."
> Intestate, 1429, leaving 178,221 florins *di sugello*,
> As is said in Cosimo's red leather note book. Di sugello. (21/96)

Through the dry dates and sums, the document breathes with the smug power of a Tiresian voice, and the "Di sugello" seal affixed to his legacy reinforces Giovanni's advice to his sons to stick to business.

Lorenzo listens to the voice of Cosimo, who so successfully followed his father's advice that he could mock those citizens who cut Giovanni and boast that he can "cut" all the "Honest citizens" he wants out of the "red cloth" which alone distinguishes aristocrats. He then skims fragments that record Cosimo's control of credit—which could break cities or force truces just by calling in loans—but he recalls, too, how his own father, Piero, like the sorcerer's apprentice, nearly destroyed himself and the Medici empire by trying the same maneuver. On the advice of the treacherous "Diotisalvi" Neroni, "Piero called in the credits" (21/96) and set off a chain of bankruptcies that

turned Florence against the Medici and nearly got him "like to be murdered."
As Piero was returning to Florence, assassins lay in ambush for him, and when
"young Lauro came down ahead of him, in the road," they asked if Piero were
behind him. "Yes, father is coming," Lorenzo coolly replied, then sent word
back to Piero to take another route home.

As that same cool voice reflects on Piero's legacy,

> Intestate, '69, in December, leaving me 237,989 florins,
> As you will find in my big green account book
> In carta di capretto   (21/96)

What Lorenzo relishes most in his own affairs and in those of his ancestors is
the Medici combination of power and patronage. Inspired by Gemisthus
Plethon at the Council of Ferrara-Florence, Cosimo "caught the young boy
Ficino / And had him taught the greek language" (21/96). In Canto 23 Pound
places Ficino's translations in a long chain of textual transmissions that shaped
the Renaissance:

> "Et omniformis," Psellos, "omnis
> "Intellectus est." God's fire. Gemisto:
> "Never with this religion
> "Will you make men of the greeks.
> "But build wall across Peloponesus
> "And organize, and...
>   damn these Eyetalian barbarians."
> And Novvy's ship went down in the tempest
> Or at least they chucked the books overboard.   (23/107)

The opening phrase, asserting that every intellect is capable of assuming every
shape, comes from Ficino's Latin translation of third-century Greek Neopla-
tonist Porphyry.[8] Ficino himself is proof of the principle of intellectual
metamorphosis that he celebrates, since, as a translator, he is assuming the
shape of Porphyry—himself a polymath whose ideas were reshapings of other
intellects. Porphyry, in turn, was metamorphosed by his pupil Iamblichus, who
translated the Neoplatonic "One" into the vivid mythological image of "God's
fire," and in the eleventh century Neoplatonism was itself renewed by the
Byzantine philosopher "Psellos" and transplanted to Italy by "Gemisto"
Plethon, whose lectures inspired Cosimo de Medici to sponsor Ficino's Greek
lessons and whose manuscripts Pound came across "in the Laurenziana in
Firenze."[9] Thus, the economy of the Medicis conserved the wealth of the
classical past and redeemed such losses as Novello Malatesta's shipload of
Greek manuscripts and Plethon's dream of a revived Greek culture on the
Peloponnesus.

Where Plethon's dream flowers is Lorenzo's Florence; from there, as Pound shows with another document, it is transplanted into the New World:

> "Could you", wrote Mr. Jefferson,
> "Find me a gardener
> Who can play the french horn?
> The bounds of American fortune
> Will not admit the indulgence of a domestic band of
> Musicians, yet I have thought that a passion for music
> Might be reconciled with that economy which we are
> Obliged to observe. (21/97)

By placing this letter from Thomas Jefferson to Giovanni Fabroni in the middle of Lorenzo's account books, Pound traces another metamorphosis of the classical past. The contrast between Lorenzo Medici's brusque shorthand and Jefferson's elegant longhand resolves in their mutual concern with the harmony between civic economy and artistic creation. While neither Venice nor Ferrara could maintain that balance, Lorenzo, who died in the same year that America was discovered, strikes it in Florence, and Jefferson, with his project for an economical chamber orchestra built of "renaissance" laborers, imports the same dream of civic and artistic order into America. In the next block of Cantos, Pound will trace its growth and decay in his native soil.

V

Presidential Correspondence

It may have been a birthday present from T. S. Eliot—the Memorial Edition of Thomas Jefferson's letters—that prompted Pound to render the flowering of American culture through the papers of four American presidents: Jefferson, John Adams, John Quincy Adams, and Martin Van Buren. All of these documents, he believed, had been suppressed by the historical black-out: John Quincy Adams's *Diary* and Martin Van Buren's *Autobiography* had been out of print for years; the expense of the Jefferson Memorial Edition and the ten volumes of John Adams's papers kept these works out of wide circulation.[1] By condensing and "making new" these presidential papers, Pound thought he was combating the black-out and the usurious forces he saw behind it. Those forces had taken root in America around the National Bank, and the image of that bank looms behind all of these "Presidential Cantos" (Cantos 31 through 34, and Canto 38). The bank finally emerges in Canto 38 when its charter comes up for renewal, and, though that document was defeated in 1836, glimpses of twentieth-century munitions-makers and financiers frequently remind us that the forces of usury did not stay dead. On the other hand, interwoven images of the ancient world, Provence, and Renaissance Italy suggest that America in the age of Jefferson and Andrew Jackson was a metamorphosis of the culture that Pound has traced through the first thirty Cantos.

The challenge of condensing and making new the mass of presidential papers drove Pound to employ an intricate strategy of verbal and visual play in order to weave his documentary shards into a poetic collage. In Canto 31, for example, while he seems to be skipping at random through Jefferson's correspondence, which is as much a rag-bag of letters as is Malatesta's post-bag, these fragments coalesce around what Pound called Jefferson's "canalization of America."[2] One of the first letters, which Jefferson wrote to Washington when he was ambassador to France, is quite literally concerned with building a canal:

"I remember having written you while Congress sat at Annapolis,
"on water communication between ours and the western
        country,
"particularly the information...of the plain between
"Big Beaver and Cayohoga, which made me hope that a canal
......navigation of Lake Erie and the Ohio. You must have had
"occasion of getting better information on this subject
"and if you have you wd. oblige me
"by a communication of it. I consider this canal,
"if practicable, as a very important work.
>   T.J. to General Washington, 1787   (31/153)

The western canal Jefferson envisions becomes a metaphor for the channels of communication, opened up by his letters, between old world and new, past and present.

Jefferson's letters trace his efforts to "canalize" America by circulating antislavery pamphlets, crossing Old and New World plants, and promoting inventions like the proto-submarine developed by "a countryman of ours, Mr Bushnell of Connecticut" (31/153). As a connector and propeller himself, Jefferson provided "passage" for Thomas Paine between America and Europe, and tried to clear the "port of France" of monopolistic blockage that "absorbs too much" (31/154) from free trade with American tobacco farmers. As ambassador to France, he sent President Madison a coded message that France was on the brink of bankruptcy; he then rechanneled American debts to the more solvent—and canalized—Holland. Turning the metaphor again, Pound quotes from a late letter from Jefferson to his nephew Dabney Carr about the importance of colonial committees of correspondence for the American Revolution. Such committees, Jefferson recalls, created a "channel of correspondence" (31/156) among the fragmented colonies and helped canalize them into a new nation.

In art, too, Jefferson carefully regulated the flow of the European past into the new American world by recommending that Washington choose "modern dress" (31/153) instead of the obligatory toga for his statue. On the other hand, he urged a vital making new of classical culture by recommending the "Maison Quarrée" as a model for the Capitol building in Richmond. Since the Maison Quarrée was itself a restored Roman temple (with Corinthian columns), its translation to America would constitute another instance, like the Tempio, of the architectural metamorphosis of the classical world. Like Malatesta, as well as Odysseus—who in Canto 1 corresponded with the past by digging an "ell-square pitkin" (1/3)—Jefferson was a "canalizer" who preserved the flow of vital documents from the past into the present. One of his strangest projects sounds like *The Cantos* itself—a collage of passages cut out from the Gospels that he planned to amplify with Greek, Latin, and French translations and then "subjoin Gosindi's Syntagma / of the doctrines of Epicurus" (31/156).[3]

What blocks the free flow of such cross-cultural and transhistorical canalizing is the historical black-out epitomized by Jefferson's archenemy, Alexander Hamilton, the "prime SNOT" in American history. Another channel-clogger is "Mr Robert Smith" (31/154), Jefferson's navy secretary and Madison's secretary of state, whose inept handling of foreign correspondence and whose attacks on Treasury Secretary Albert Gallatin impeded the flow of government business. Equally damning (and damning) are European aristocrats, like Lafayette, with his gross "ignorance of government and history" (31/155), and "English papers" with "their lies" (31/154) about economic conditions in America. Guilty also is the "church of St. Peter" (31/156), which has falsified not only sacred but also secular documents. In a letter to John Adams, Jefferson explains how a mistranslation of the phrase "en ancien scripture" (in ancient writing) as "*Holy Scripture*" (31/156), by a legal commentator in the time of Henry VI, has perpetuated a ridiculous conflation of civic and ecclesiastical law throughout British history.[4]

The economic analogue for this blockage of textual channels is usury:

> "But observe that the public were at the same time paying
> on it an interest of exactly the same amount
> (four million dollars). Where then is the gain to either
> party which makes it a public blessing?"
> to Mr Eppes, 1813   (31/155)

Writing to his son-in-law, Congressman Eppes, Jefferson attacked the proposal for a National Bank that Congress was considering in 1813, pointing out that such a bank would only saddle America with usurious interest payments. By placing the bank's charter amid these other images, Pound signals its emergence, in these Presidential Cantos, as the central document of blockage and waste in early America.

Two of America's greatest canalizers, Jefferson and Adams, themselves had to overcome the blockage of political bickering to renew their friendship in old age. Prompted by a mutual friend, the former presidents put aside their differences and began corresponding in 1812. Their letters, Pound thought, constitute a monumental document of American culture, a philosophical canal between Massachusetts and Virginia that parallels the revolutionary committees of correspondence. From these and other letters Pound generates more metaphors for channels of correspondence, such as "the Amphitrite" (32/157), a French ship that secretly supplied American troops during the Revolution, and "*Monsieur Saint-Libin*," a man "well-versed in languages" who opened relations between France and East Indian princes who were opposed to British rule. Aaron Burr, on the other hand, is seen as a false canalizer who really "had / no interest in the Ohio canal" (32/157) but used it as a pretext to plot a rebellion against the American government.

Jefferson's canalizing projects ranged from the cultivation of imported ani-
mals and hybrid plants to the opening of diplomatic channels with "Emperor
(Alexander)" of Russia. One significant project involved "type-founding"
(32/158) so that America need not depend upon English printers for books. To
acquire "antimony," which "is essential" for printing, Jefferson sent Philadel-
phian printer "Mr Ronaldson" to Spain, a mission that recalls Soncinus'
acquisition of "greek fonts" and "chancellry letters" (30/148). Like Malatesta's
"inky" fonts (10/44) and Odysseus' flowing "fosse" (1/3), these printing canals
channel the flow of classical texts into the New World, even to the American
Indians, since Jefferson's plans for "civilizing the indians" included teaching
"writing, to / keep accounts" and reading, through such texts as "Aesop's
Fables" (32/158).

In their letters, too, Jefferson and Adams rage against the forces that block
such canalizing. Writing to William Johnson, who was compiling a history of
American political parties, Jefferson castigates the Monarchist party, which,
like its European prototypes, believes it necessary to oppress the masses "by
hard labour, poverty, ignorance" (32/158). The "Cannibals of Europe are
eating one another again" (32/159), Jefferson writes bitterly to Adams, who,
in turn, supplies a grotesque parody of his correspondence with Jefferson:

> Louis Sixteenth was a fool
> The King of Spain was a fool, the King of Naples a fool
> they despatched two couriers weekly to tell each other, over a
>   thousand miles
>   what they had killed...   (32/159)

European hogs, cannibals, gluttons, and other figures of blockage have their
American counterparts in an American quartermaster whose "long letters"
(33/160) of red tape only clog the flow of supplies to the revolutionary army.
Similarly, "Judge Marshall" with his frequent digressions "out of his case, to say
what the law in a moot case would be" (32/159), clogs America's legal
channels.

All of this blockage and black-out furthers the historical conspiracy that
John Adams describes at the opening of Canto 33, a "despotism" that either
destroys or corrupts "all records" (33/160). Already, Adams laments, "the
funding and banking system" is at work distorting history by elevating the
image of Washington to detract attention from the ideas of other American
patriots (33/162). Pound identifies this despotism with the usurious ring of
financiers, arms-makers, politicians, journalists, priests, and academics who
suppress documents in the "printing-house of hell." Jefferson and Adams both
suspected a similar historical black-out behind the mass illiteracy of European
peasants—another conspiracy to prevent the free circulation of ideas that

sparked the American Revolution. Their suspicions prompt Pound to cut away from the Adams-Jefferson letters to Marx's *Das Kapital*:

> (Das Kapital) denounced in 1842 still
> continue (today 1864) report of '42 was merely
> chucked into the archives and remained there while
> these boys were ruined and became fathers of this
> generation...for workshops remained a dead letter
> down to 1871 when was taken from control of municipal...
> and placed in hands of the factory inspectors, to
> whose body they added eight (8) assistants to deal with
> over one hundred thousand workshops and over 300 tile
> yards.   (33/162)

Here Marx quotes from an 1864 report on British factory conditions which, in turn, digs up an earlier document—an 1842 report by a parliamentary commission on child labor practices that had been suppressed while the hideous conditions persisted and had produced a second generation of illiterate children to be exploited by their parents and the factory owners. Into this palimpsest of suppressed documents Pound weaves another blacked-out text—the Workshop Regulations Act of 1871 that remained a "dead letter" because its enforcement was left to local authorities. Even after Parliament created national inspectors, the document was still subverted by providing only "eight (8)" inspectors for the 100,000 workshops.

Pound includes another document from *Das Kapital*, a letter from "Lord H. de Walden," the British minister to Brussels, who describes his conversation with the Belgian minister about similar difficulties in getting child-labor legislation past the usurers who "met any law tampering with the absolute freedom of labor" with "jealous uneasiness" (33/162). Another document, the British Factory Act "of 1848," met the same fate when its inspectors were "denounced" by capitalists as "a species of revolutionary commissar pitilessly sacrificing the unfortunate labourers to their humanitarian fantasies" (33/162-63). A corollary to that act, sponsored by "John Hobhouse" in 1849, tried to close one of its loopholes by forbidding factory owners and their relatives from sitting as magistrates on "cases concerning the spinning of cotton" (33/163). The difficulty of fighting the usurers, however, is illustrated by an excerpt from another report, by "Leonard Horner," for a commission on child labor, describing the factory owners' trick of shifting children "from one factory to another" to outwit the inspectors (33/163).

From Marx's description of nineteenth-century subversion, Pound moves into the twentieth century with Grigory Bessedovsky's *Revelations of a Soviet Diplomat*. Bessedovsky's memoirs contain secret documents that revealed

Stalin's plans to fund a German revolution and overthrow Chiang Kai-shek in China. Bessedovsky also describes the clogging of diplomatic channels by Soviet ambassadors, who had to distort their reports to comply with "what theories are in fashion in Moscow" (33/163). Such diplomats even worked hand-in-hand with the capitalists denounced by Marx, reaping huge profits by conspiring with British bankers to discount Soviet bills. Having traced the workings of the historical black-out across Europe in the nineteenth and twentieth centuries, Pound returns to America at the end of Canto 33 and focuses on the usurious center of that documentary suppression. The National Bank that Jefferson and Adams warned against and that John Quincy Adams and Martin Van Buren helped to defeat was resurrected in the twentieth century as the Federal Reserve Board. Quoting from a speech by Senator Brookhart of Iowa in 1931, a speech that Pound celebrated as "the most important historical document of the period that I have come upon," Pound reveals the entrenchment of usury in the New World.[5] Brookhart (whose name links him to other canalizers) calls for an investigation into the Reserve Board's suppression and distortion of information that helped to bring on the Depression. The directors of the board withheld from small businesses and the public its imminent decision to increase railroad rates and discount loans, but they leaked this crucial information to large corporations like "Swiftamoursinclair" (33/164) whose bankers were board members themselves. Outraged that Brookhart's speech was not being circulated in the newspapers, Pound excerpted it in *The Cantos* as part of his own struggle against the historical black-out.

Canto 34 opens with a conversation between Jefferson and Dr. Samuel Mitchell, recorded in the *Diary of John Quincy Adams*:

> Oils, beasts, grasses, petrifications, birds, incrustations,
> Dr. Mitchell's conversation was various.....   (34/165)

The conversation occurred in 1807, shortly before John Quincy Adams embarked as minister to Russia to maintain the channel of communication that Jefferson had opened "with the Emperor (Alexander)" (32/157). Adams's *Diary*, Pound believed, was another victim of the historical black-out, which delayed its publication until 1928, and this suppression contributed to the general ignorance among most Americans of John Quincy Adams. To combat that ignorance, Pound condensed the *Diary* and wove it into strands of his canal metaphor. This opening conversation, for example, displays the many-mindedness of Dr. Mitchell and presents another instance of free-flowing channels of information, while the "petrifactions" and "incrustations" suggest the blockage that impedes canalization.

As minister to Russia, John Quincy Adams soon found himself bogged down in diplomatic channels, and, instead of the many-sided conversation of Jefferson and Dr. Mitchell, he encountered only a few diplomats, like Russian Minister Count Romanzoff, "who have any interest in literature, conversation" (34/165). Pound ties Adams's relish for such conversation to his work on a treaty that will cut through British and French trade restrictions and give American ships "Freedom of admission . . . freedom of departure, freedom of purchase and sale" (34/165). Adams's attempts to canalize trade were matched by Count Romanzoff, who offered to act as mediator between England and America in the War of 1812 but received an "answer" from England that blocked his efforts (34/166). When peace negotiations did open, Adams had to fight not only the British ministers but also his co-negotiators "Mr Gallatin, / Mr Bayard" to preserve the rights of American boats "in Florida," "on the Mississippi," and "off Newfoundland" (34/166).

When he returned to America, Adams, as Madison's secretary of state, worked to preserve those open channels of conversation and commerce. With the help of Spanish Minister "Onis," (34/167) he acquired Florida from Spain, despite widespread public resentment, and, with the British minister, "Mr Bagot," he negotiated an arms-limitation treaty on the Great Lakes "for the tranquillity of this country" (34/167). From his conversation with William Jackson, who had taken minutes at the Constitutional Convention, Adams learned that James Madison "was very efficient" in channeling that great document through the waters of warring political factions.

Against these canalizers, however, stood the forces of "Tammany Hall" (34/167), which Adams encountered on his return from Europe: "Gouverneur Morris and Mr / Astor," who feted Adams on his way through New York, and DeWitt Clinton

> Never more low and discredited
> Than just before being elected (comma)
> Without opposition (comma) Governor of New York State.   (34/167)

Adams found a more widespread and pernicious "discrediting" among the nation's banks that were "breaking all over the country, / Some in a sneaking, some in an impertinent manner" (34/167), clogging the flow of money with their glut of "Paper currency" and accumulating "debts as long as credit can be strained" (34/168). Retracing the same vicious circle of usury outlined in the Hell Cantos, Pound cuts to Adams's record of his conversation with President Monroe about the insidious links between financiers, politicians, and journalists:

> Jan 18th. 1820. I (J.Q.A.) called at the President's
> And the President said: Colonel Johnson
> might have been more worthily occupied than in acting as
> medium for proposal of
> furnishing ten thousand stand of arms to Venezuela
> in order to make a job for Duane.   (34/167)

The insidious conduit here is Senator Richard Johnson of Kentucky, who rigged a deal for selling arms to South America so that his agent, William Duane, editor of a newspaper that Adams once described as the "most slanderous" in the country, could reap a profit.

Returning to the Ohio canal envisioned by Jefferson at the opening of Canto 31, Pound describes President John Quincy Adams's encounter with his attorney general, William Wirt. Wirt had been retained privately by the Baltimore Railway Company to help it fight the Ohio Canal Company. When he asked Adams if taking such a case would involve a conflict of interest, the president thundered that it certainly would "Interfere with official duty" (34/169). Adams fought the railway company's efforts to block the canal and argued that "the U.S. was interested in / the Canal Company by their subscription of one million dollars" (34/169). By continuing Jefferson's dream of a canal linking "Lake Erie and the Ohio" (31/153), Adams stands as a vital figure of continuity, transmission, and communication in the project of "canalizing" America into an incarnation of that civic paradise glimpsed briefly in the Venice of Canto 17, a canal-knitted metamorphosis of Aphrodite.

Aphrodite's human incarnations as man- and city-destroying women like Helen or Eleanor of Aquitaine emerge in the scandal of "Mrs Eaton" (34/169), which rocked the first term of Adams's successor, Andrew Jackson. Peggy Eaton was the wife of Jackson's secretary of war, and rumors spread that her affair with Eaton had brought on the death of her first husband. She was ostracized by Washington society, and "Mrs Calhoun," wife of Jackson's vice-president, "remained in the untainted atmosphere" (34/169) of South Carolina rather than mingle with Mrs. Eaton in Washington. Jackson, whose own wife had been the victim of scandal, defended Peggy, as did his secretary of state, Martin Van Buren, but the affair clogged the administration and Eaton finally had to resign.

Culling fragments from Adams's *Diary*, Pound suggests that the scandal was engineered by usurers, who were alarmed by Jackson's threats against the National Bank. When former president Adams returned to "seat Number 203" in Congress, he went to the director of the National Bank and closed out his account:

> I called upon Nicholas Biddle...and recd. two dividends
> of my bank stock.....as I might be called to take part in
> public measures.....I wished to divest myself
> of all personal interest....Nov. 9. '31. (34/169)

Another act of the elder statesman was to reopen communications with President Jackson by clearing up a misunderstanding that had blocked their "social / intercourse"(34/170)—rumors, similar to those in the Peggy Eaton scandal, that Adams had once slandered Mrs. Jackson. These metaphors for canalizing turn especially playful as Pound excerpts Adams's remarks on meeting Harriet Martineau:

> Miss Martineau....author of *Conversations upon Political Economy*
> ..a young woman...deaf..and hearing only through an ear-
>   trumpet
> Her conversation is lively and easy.... (34/170)

In contrast to the "shallow speeches of "Mr. Clay, Mr. Calhoun, Mr. Webster," the conversational canal with Harriet Martineau runs to the deep issues of political economy.

Pound concludes his portrait of Adams with the old man's congressional battle against the "gag rule" that blocked all debate on slavery. Under this rule, all petitions against slavery were merely placed on a table in the House chamber without being discussed or printed. Adams's most strenuous efforts at canalizing were directed against this black-out: he introduced hundreds of antislavery petitions, only to see them silently laid on the table; every time he stood to speak out against slavery, he was shouted down by the Speaker and other congressmen. Against such a black-out he could only lament:

> The world, the flesh, the devils in hell are
> Against any man who now in the North American Union
> shall dare to join the standard of Almighty God to
> Put down the African slave trade...what can I
> Seventy-four years, verge of my birthday, shaking hand
> ...for the suppression of the African slave trade..... (34/170-71)

In these lines Pound plays with an ironic reversal of his central metaphor: Adams fights the gag rule in order to open a channel of communication, but what he seeks to do is suppress and block the insidious canal of slavery between America and Africa.

Adams ultimately did break through the gag rule to propose an amendment to the Constitution that would make representation "Proportioned to free inhabitants (Dec. 21. '43)" (34/171). The date of that breakthrough was inscribed on a cane made from a timber of the *Constitution* and presented to Adams by his constituents. Adams turned the cane over to the U.S. Patent Office, and Pound cleverly rhymes that gift with the "Electro-magnetic (Morse)" patent as documents of free communication. These final images surround a journey Adams took in 1843 to Buffalo, Rochester, Lake Erie, Cincinnati, and the Ohio Valley—the area Jefferson envisioned at the opening of Canto 31 as a network of canals. On his odyssey Adams is greeted by a "Firemen's torchlight procession" (31/171) similar to the parade that honored Malatesta on his return from Greece (11/51). The flowing parade symbolizes Jefferson's dream of enlightenment and cultural transmission.

The next great American canalizer Pound takes up is Martin Van Buren, who wrote his memoirs in Italy in the 1850s.[6] Working "from many documents and from memory," the former president retraced the battle over the charter of the National Bank. Although Van Buren, Andrew Jackson, Thomas Hart Benton, and others managed to block renewal of the charter, the usurious forces behind the document did not die. They were responsible, Pound believed, for "the general indefinite wobble" of the modern world (35/173) and for the fact that "Van Buren's memoirs stayed six decades in manuscript," until 1905, when they were presented to the Library of Congress.[7] Still, the memoirs were not published until 1918, and even then only as the *Annual Report of the American Historical Commission*. Pound did not hear of the *Autobiography* until 1932, the same year that another long-buried document was published: " 'Peggy Eaton's own story' (Headline 1932)" (37/181). Pound is quoting a newspaper headline announcing the publication of Peggy Eaton's *Autobiography*, which supported his belief that the Washington scandal over "the standard of feminine virtue" was trumped up to force Eaton and Van Buren out of Jackson's cabinet. Van Buren's cavalier defense of Peggy Eaton rhymes with Cavalcanti's celebration of another metamorphosis of Aphrodite in "Donna mi priegha," which Pound translates in Canto 36.

The first excerpts Pound takes from Van Buren's *Autobiography* extend the parallel between America and Italy by recalling Cunizza's articles of manumission that inspired both Cavalcanti and Dante:

> "Thou shalt not," said Martin Van Buren, "jail 'em for debt."
> "that an immigrant shd. set out with good banknotes
> and find 'em at the end of his voyage
> but waste paper....if a man have in primeval forest
> set up his cabin, shall rich patroon take it from him?   (37/181)

Like Cunizza, Jefferson, and John Quincy Adams, Van Buren worked against slavery, this time the slavery of usury perpetrated by banks and wealthy landowners against immigrants and small farmers. As a state senator of New

York, he introduced bills prohibiting the jailing of debtors, and as governor in 1829 he forced banks to insure their notes against failure. As a U.S. senator, in 1826 he worked to keep state and local affairs free from the clogging intrusions of the federal government. He opposed Supreme Court interference with the states, noting that the "High judges" are as "subject to passions" and "esprit de corps" as other men (37/181). Similarly, he fought federal control of canals and roads, for, "when a turnpike depends upon congress / local supervision is lost" (37/182). In the same Jeffersonian spirit, Van Buren worked for an "extension of franchise" (37/181) to all taxpaying citizens, saying that "Two words" that "came in with" the American Revolution were "taxation" and "representation."

He identified the greatest impediment to America's growth and vitality, however, in the corrupt documents of usury that oppress the

> working classes
>   who mostly
> have no control over paper, and
> derive no profit from bank stock..... (37/182)

As vice-president and president, he fought against the financial powers —the "merchants" who "will not confess over trading"; the "speculators" who deny their "disposition to speculate"; and the politicians, like "Mr Clay," who clogged Van Buren's efforts to dispense government "land / to actual settler" (37/182).

Of all the documents of usury, however, it was the charter of the National Bank that posed the greatest threat to the new nation. Pound recounts the battle over renewing the charter, from President Jackson's first assault in his inaugural address in 1829, through the congressional debates that eventually killed the charter in 1836, to the election of 1840, when Van Buren was defeated in his bid for reelection by "Tip an' Tyler" (37/183) and by, Pound suggests, the financial interests. Cutting back and forth through Van Buren's memoirs of these years, Pound extracts snatches of voices speaking for and against the charter. On the one hand, we hear Henry Clay and Daniel Webster intoning the virtues of "Banking corporations" where the "interests of the rich and the poor are happily blended" (37/182). On the other hand, we hear the colloquial drawl of Jackson, asserting, "No where so well deposited as in the pants of the people, / Wealth ain't" (37/182). Van Buren himself debunks Clay's grandiloquence by asking the senator, after a particularly fulsome speech, for "A pinch of your excellent Maccoby snuff" (37/182).

Although the charter was not scheduled to come up for renewal until 1836, Jackson's election in 1828 frightened the bank's supporters and prompted its president, Nicholas Biddle, to meet with Jackson. Either through astounding

naiveté or because of Jackson's shrewd diplomacy, Biddle came away feeling
that the charter was safe. Pound quotes excerpts from two of Biddle's
letters—one to Robert Lenox, head of the New York Chamber of Commerce,
and the other to Alexander Hamilton—to illustrate Biddle's false sense of
security:

> "Friendly feeling toward our bank in
> "the mind of the President (Jackson
> whose autograph was sent to the Princess Victoria)
>   wrote Biddle to Lennox Dec. 1829
> "Counter rumours without foundation, I had
> "a full and frank talk with the President who was
> "most kind about its (the bank's) services to the country"
>   Biddle to Hamilton in November.   (37/183)

It soon became clear, however, that Jackson would use his "veto power" to
defeat renewal of the charter, and Biddle was "Authorized" to "use funds at /
discretion (its funds, his discretion)" to wage a press campaign against
Jackson's reelection.

This characteristic link between usurious financiers and the "press gang" was
extended by Biddle's move to increase drastically the bank's "line of discounts"
so that failure to renew the charter would rain financial disaster on busi-
nessmen and property-owners in debt to the bank, most of whom were in the
Middle West, where Jackson had his strongest support. It was this threat of
panic that Daniel Webster, himself one of the bank's greatest debtors and
supporters, used in the Senate to try to muster enough votes to override
Jackson's veto of the charter. The veto stood, however, and the charter was
not renewed even though the bank pulled out all the stops in the fight:
"deranging the country's credits, obtaining by panic / control over public
mind," "controlling government's funds / to the betrayal of the nation,"
"obstructing the government," "acting in illegal secret," "pouring oil on the
press, / giving nominal loans on inexistent security," (37/184) and nearly
breaking all of the city banks of New York by calling in its credits until Treasury
Secretary "Mr Taney" (37/185) halted the collection and transferred cash to
state banks.

When Van Buren took office in 1837, he faced enormous pressure to extend
the charter; he refused, however, even in the face of a financial panic that was
precipitated, Pound believed, by the bank. Instead of resurrecting the charter,
he tried to create an independent treasury with "revenue for wants of the
government / to be kept under public control" (37/182). The price he paid for
his continued fight against the charter was the defamation of his own character
by accusations that he was a "dough-face" who supported slavery and a

"profligate" who, like Doge Selvo's wife, "brought in the vice of luxuria" (37/183) by eating with golden forks ("aureis furculis"). Although he did manage to prevent a renewal of the bank charter, Van Buren's loss in the election of 1840 signaled a victory for the forces of usury, who would, as Pound saw it, completely take over the American economy after the Civil War. Although the National Bank would never be chartered again, the Federal Reserve System, which Pound considered a comparable evil, appeared as its metamorphosis.

Near the end of Canto 38, Pound interjects the dateline of Van Buren's memoirs, "Sorrento, June 21st. Villa Falangola / In the vicinage of Vesuvius" (37/185). The image of the old president in retirement in Italy returns Pound to the earlier setting and provides a transition to the next block of documentary Cantos, which focus on another bank charter, for the Monte dei Paschi (Bank of the Pastures) in Siena. The image also relates Van Buren's reflections "in the mirror of memory" to the buried force of Vesuvius, blocked from publication but promising, if released, to destroy the usurious wasteland of the modern world. While Pound's suspicions of usury and the historical black-out of presidential papers may seem like paranoiac fantasy, they gain some credibility when we find a contemporary economic historian, John Kenneth Galbraith, speculating about the suppression of American monetary history. Galbraith observes how little the general public knows about the economic views of the founding fathers and ponders the strange gentlemen's agreement among economic historians to ignore the successful monetary experiments of the Middle Colonies, one of which, Maryland, enacted a program of government dividends that Galbraith himself compares to the Social Credit proposals of Pound's favorite economist, Major Douglas.[8]

VI

Sienese Bank Charters

In *The Fifth Decad of Cantos* (Cantos 42-51) Pound drew on documents he found in a nine-volume work compiled by Narciso Mengozzi entitled *Il Monte dei Paschi di Siene e le Aziende in Esso Riunite.*[1] The documents trace the history of a "damn good bank" (42/209), the Monte dei Paschi (Bank of the Pastures), founded in Siena in the seventeenth century and still operating today. For Pound, the Monte was the model for a healthy "species of bank"—"not yet a banco di giro" (42/209) earning interest by rotating money through its various accounts, but a bank whose wealth was founded upon the earth itself and whose profits went back into the community to alleviate poverty and promote the arts. Angry because newspapers would not publish these vital documents even in the face of a worldwide depression, Pound transmitted them through *The Cantos*, hoping that they might stimulate economic reform. He even went to the Sienese archives to examine notaries' copies of the papers Mengozzi collected, stressing actual contact with the documents by reproducing their seals, abbreviations, and even their shelf numbers:

> 1251 of the Protocols marked also
> X,I,I,F, and four arabic   (43/216)

As George Kearns has observed, we find in these Cantos a dramatization of Pound's "activity in the archives," a "mimesis of the act of research itself, of someone skimming through documents."[2]

The inclusion of the Monte charters seems to answer Thomas Jefferson's plea for "OUR bank, own bank"—not a bank like the National Bank but our *own* bank that we *own* to insure "Independent use of money (our OWN)" (40/197). While the Sienese charters fulfill Jefferson's hopes, they clash with documents that mark the usurpation of public land and wealth by private usurers: an oil lease from the Shah of Persia to "THE MOST GLORIOUS MR. / D'ARCY" (40/197); an 1860 congressional "report of committee" (40/197),

revealing John Pierpont Morgan's influence on the federal government; and
the "Pujo investigation" (40/198) report that fifty years later traced the
unchecked growth of Morgan's power. Another documentary juxtaposition
equates the Monte charters with an ancient document that opened up a new
world—*The Periplus of Hanno*, the record of a Carthaginian voyage around the
northwest coast of Africa in 470 B.C.:

> PLEASING TO CARTHEGENIANS: HANNO
>
> that he ply beyond pillars of Herakles
> 60 ships of armada to lay out Phoenecian cities
> to each ship 50 oars, in all
> 30 thousand aboard them with water, wheat in provision.
> Two days beyond Gibel Tara layed in the wide plain
> Thumiatehyon, went westward to Solois
> an headland covered with trees
> Entha hieron Poseidōnos, against the sun half a day
> is seabord marshland high-murmuring rushes.   (40/199)

This fragmentary text is an obvious parallel to Odysseus' voyage in Canto 1,
and, just as Odysseus and Hanno are "seeking an exit" from the known world,
Pound is searching for an escape from the modern wasteland of usury.[3] The
Monte documents point the way to a new economic world, and Pound displays
them in his poem just as the Carthaginians "hung" Hanno's *Periplus* "with his
map in their temple" (40/201).

Pound's display constitutes a documentary triptych woven through Cantos
42 and 43. The first document reflects the Sienese request in 1619 for "A
mount, a bank, a fund a bottom" for their impoverished community (42/209).
Since Siena was then a duchy of Florence, the Sienese Collegio de Balia
(which Pound calls "the Bailey") made its request to the grand duke of
Tuscany, young Ferdinando II, who ruled under the tutelage of his mother, the
Grand Duchess Maria Maddalena of Austria, and his grandmother, the Grand
Duchess Maria Christina of Lorraine. Ferdinando was also instructed by a
special Florentine council, and the second document in Pound's triptych is the
council's recommendation, in 1622, that Duke Ferdinand underwrite the
bank, provided that Siena agree to certain regulations. At first the Sienese
balked, but they finally accepted the conditions, and on November 2, 1624 the
agreement between the grand duke of Tuscany and the Sienese people was
formally signed, chartering the Monte dei Paschi.

Beginning with Siena's plea for a bank of its own, Pound interweaves these
three documents, punning on "mount," "bank," "fund," "species," and
"damn" to link the financial institution with mountains, earthworks, and

other natural images. That organic order is reflected, too, in the regulations
governing the Monte:

> as third, a Yearly balance
> as 5th that any citizen shall have right to deposit
> and to fruits therefrom resultant at five percent annual interest
> and that borrowers pay a bit over that
> for services (dei ministri) that is for running expenses   (42/209)

Pound plays the "bureaucratese" of the document—"fruits therefrom result-
ant"—against the colloquial twang of "a bit over that" and "running expenses"
to get the flavor of the old text as well as the ghostly voices buried beneath it.
The ten regulations quietly rhyme with the Ten Commandments, as Pound
simulates the seal and signature of the notary public of Siena:

> July 1623
> Loco Signi
> +   [a cross in the margin]
> That profit on deposits should be used to cover all losses
> and the distributions on the fifth year be made from remaining
> profits, after restoration of losses no (benché) matter how
> small
> with sane small reserve against future idem
> I, Livio Pasquini, notary, citizen of Siena, most faithfully copied
> July 18th. 1623
> Consules, Iudices, and notary public pro serenissimo
> attest Livio's superscript next date being November.
>   wave falls and the hand falls
> Thou shalt not always walk in the sun
>   or see weed sprout over cornice
> Thy work in set space of years, not over an hundred.   (42/210)

The biblical "Thou shalt not," the image of words carved in stone, and the
sealed vow of Livio, who faithfully copied these ten commandments, transfig-
ure the council report into a new covenant by which a community generates
credit and garners interest from its own land—a harvest underscored by
Pound's play on the Italian word for 'interest,' *frutto*.[4]

Pound then turns to the Florentine council report that urges Grand Duke
Ferdinand and his guardians to grant the Sienese request to replace their old
bank, the Monte dei Pietà, which could only lend money on collateral, with a
new bank that could create and extend credit:

> That the Mount of Pity (or Hock Shop)
> municipal of Siena has lent only on pledges
> that is on stuff actually hocked...wd be we believe useful
> and beneficent that there be place to lend licitly
> MONEY to receive licitly money
> at moderate and legitimate interest   (42/210)

In actuality, the Monte dei Pietà was not separate from the Monte dei Paschi and had already begun extending credit to local farmers by 1610, but Pound creates a symbolic contrast between the two banks with a pun linking the "Mount of Pity" to the "Pity" (30/147) denounced by Artemis in Canto 30:

> Compleynt, compleynt I hearde upon a day,
> Artemis singing, Artemis, Artemis
> Agaynst Pity lifted her wail:
> Pity causeth the forests to fail,
> Pity slayeth my nymphs,
> Pity spareth so many an evil thing.   (30/147)

The unnatural sentimentality of pity here has its economic analogue in the excesses of usury. Just as natural death and renewal are frustrated "on account of Pity," the gyrating accounts of usurious banks earn interest, "unnaturally," on nonexistent money.

In the Florentine report, the solemn biblical tone of the first document modulates into language that is chatty, shrewd, and—benefitting the city where the Medici rose to power—skeptically optimistic about Siena's guarantees to protect the duke's warranty of 200,000 scudi:

> and that the Grand Duke hadn't lost anything by it
> Plus a list of Sienese assets (coolish)
> Plus a lien on 'The Abundance'
> And knowing that all this is but a little
> Pledge the persons and goods of the laity
> And leave open door to other towns in the state
> who care to give similar pledges
> And that whoso puts in money shall have lots in the Monte
> that yield 5% interest
> and that these shareholders shall receive their due fruit
> And that the Gd Duke make known at Siena
> to the same deputies of the Bailey...
> but that it be separate from the Pawn Shop
> and have its own magistrates and employees
> and that YYour HHighnesses send approbation
> commanding their will, we humbly with reverence

...the 29th day of Xember 1622...
 servants of YYour HHighnesses
 Nicolo de Antille
 Horatio Gionfiglioli
 Sebastiano Cellesi   (42/211-12)

By having these calculating Florentines endorse the Monte, Pound implies that such a bank, based on the human and natural resources of a community, makes sound business sense. Although they are "coolish" on the "assets" of an impoverished Siena, the Florentines are sensible enough to see that rents from the Maremma grazing lands—the "Abundance"—will safeguard the duke's investment.

Familiar with documentary red tape from passport hassles, Pound traces with grim humor the course of the Florentine report. First it goes to "TTheir HHighnesses," the duke's mother and grandmother, who give their "approbation," but then a snag develops when the report "Needs a stamp" and must be rechanneled to another member of the Florentine consulting committee, "Fabbizio" Colloredo (42/212). Pound mangles Colloredo's name and turns that of Orazio Ercolani into a growl—"Cenzio Grcolini"—to signal his own frustration at these seventeenth-century bureaucratic snags, yet he roundly approves the provision that interest from the Monte be based on purchases of "lots" of pasture land—"Loca Montis" (42/214)—since, as Giuseppe Gagliani explains, "in the 17th century, as in Dante's time, lending for interest was considered immoral."[5] This provision, openly stated in the Monte documents, is later contrasted with a very different bank charter:

Said Paterson:
 Hath benefit of interest on all
 the moneys which it, the bank, creates out of nothing.   (46/233)

The speaker is William Paterson, founder of the Bank of England, and his words come from the prospectus that established this prototype of all usurious institutions. In contrast to the open books of the Monte, this prospectus was one that Pound had to dig for, and his efforts were matched by the "Macmillan Commission" in 1929—"about two hundred and forty years / LATE"—that in its investigation into the causes of the Depression "with great difficulty got back to Paterson's / The bank makes it *ex nihil*" (46/233). This hidden document, Pound believed, exposed usurious banks that earned interest on "unnatural" money—money that existed only as figures in its ledgers. "The process by which a bank creates money out of nothing," John Kenneth Galbraith has noted, "is so simple that it repels the mind."[6] Still, few people understand it—a fact that Pound rails against as he waves the Bank of England prospectus in our faces and screams, "will any / JURY convict 'um?"(46/233).

The third Sienese document officially established the Monte dei Paschi in 1624:

> ACTUM SENIS, the
> Parish of San Joannij in the Gd Ducal Palace
> present the Marquis Joanne Christophoro   the
> illustrious Marquis Antony Mary of Malaspina
> and the most renowned Johnny something or other de Binis
> Florentine Senator, witness and I notary undersigned
> Ego Livius Pasquinus of Marius
> (deceased) filius Apostolic Imperial and Pontifical notary
> public Judge Ordinary, Citizen of Siena
> WHEREFORE
>   let all sundry and whoever be
> satisfied that the said MOUNT may be created.   (42/213)

Even though Pound stumbles over the dusty names and abbreviations, the voice of Livio Pasquini, the Sienese notary, is still heard through the dry text, telling us that he is the son of Marius, also a notary, and affixing his seal to that of the "Florentine notary public," "Nicolaus Ulivis / de Cagnascis." Pound sees these two notaries as poetic artificers whose creation, transmission, and preservation of vital documents unites them with the other heroic editors and translators in *The Cantos*.

Pound casts himself in the role of a modern Sienese notary in Canto 43 when he records a parade he witnessed in the streets of Siena:

> to the end:
>   four fat oxen
> having their arses wiped
> and in general being tidied up to serve god under my window
> with stoles of Imperial purple
> with tassels, and grooms before the carroccio
> on which carroch six lion heads
>   to receive the wax offering
> Thus arrive the gold eagles, the banners of the contrade,
> and boxes of candles
>   'Mn-YAWWH!!!'
> Said the left front ox, suddenly,
> 'pnAWH!' as they tied on his red front band   (43/216)

The parade once again testifies to the continuing vitality of a community that controls its own credit. These oxen are fat from grazing on the "Abundance," the Maremma lands whose rents also fatten the Monte's coffers and, in turn, nourish the town. The Monte thus functions as an economic canal, a font as well as a fund, which channels the fertility of nature into the community, as opposed to the unnatural blockage of usury.

After being "arse-wiped," the oxen and the parade "set off toward the Duomo" (43/217), but Pound makes the real cathedral in Siena the bank itself, describing its chartering as "the Incarnation" (43/219):

> Thus BANK of the grassland was raised into Seignory
> stati fatti Signoria, being present Paris Bolgarini
> credit of the Commune of Siena
> 12 of the Bailey present...went into committee
> I cancellarius wrote to His Highness
> A New Mount that shall receive from all sorts of persons
> from Luoghi public and private, privileged and non-privileged
> a base, a fondo, a deep, a sure and a certain
> the City having 'entrate'   (43/219)

The language and imagery here deepen the sacred character of the Monte—its twelve bailiffs, its extension of blessings to all, its rocklike base. The first supervisor, Paris Bolgarini, took the ecclesiastical title *cancellarius*, a word that goes back to the end of Canto 30 where the new printing fonts were called "chancellry" letters after the ecclesiastical script *cancellarius*. Just as the new art of printing undermined the authority of the church, so the Monte dei Paschi succeeded the church as fund and fount of communal vitality. Similarly, the bank's documents, preserved and transmitted by the notaries, could, Pound believed, become the Holy Scriptures for a new economic order.

Drawing on other documents in *Il Monte*, Pound traces the history of the bank and Siena through the eighteenth century, when Tuscany passed from Medici control to that of the Austrian house of Hapsburg-Lorraine. Under "Pietro Leopoldo" (44/223), who became grand duke of Tuscany in 1765, and his son Ferdinando, who succeeded him in 1790, decrees were issued that "made new" the Monte charters by providing Siena with economic regulation in hard times. Canto 44 opens with Pietro's decree that lifted import restrictions and cut interest rates:

> And thou shalt not, Firenze 1766, and thou shalt not
> sequestrate for debt any farm implement
> nor any yoke ox nor
> any peasant while he works with the same.   (44/223)

The biblical "Thou shalt not" echoes the original Monte charters as well as Martin Van Buren's bill to relieve debtors (37/181) in a documentary rhyme that unites America and Italy in their fight against usurers who profit from war and famine.

The need for economic regulation is further illustrated by the decrees of
Pietro's son "FERDINANDO" (42/223), who "declared against exportation /
thought grain was to eat." In honor of Ferdinando's "provident law" (44/223),
the city holds a magnificent parade like the one Pound witnessed in modern
Siena:

> Evviva Ferdinado il Terzo
> and from the contrade continued the drumming
> and blowing of trumpets and hunting horns,
> torch flares, grenades and they went to the Piazza del Duomo
> with a new hullabaloo gun shots mortaretti and pistols
> there were no streets not ablaze with the torches
> or with wood fires and straw flares   (44/224)

Still another parade celebrates a great document and culminates at the city
temple, where "four lines of tablet in marble" (43/225) commemorate
Ferdinando's decree.

Pound then contrasts this parade with a rigged ceremony held a few years
later when the French invaded Tuscany, forced Ferdinando to flee, and
gathered the Sienese around a "liberty tree" (43/225) where "citizen priest"
and "the citizen /the Archbishop" could join other "citizens" as equals. All this
revolutionary rhetoric is undercut, however, by a letter that Pound lifts from *Il
Monte*:

>   Premier Brumaire:
> Vous voudrez citoyen
> turn over all sums in yr/ cash box
> to the community, fraternité, greetings.
>   Delort
> acting for Dupont Lieutenant General
> Louis King of Etruria, Primus, absolute, without constitution.   (44/226)

Under the banner of the revolutionary calendar (the French renamed October
Brumaire) and the egalitarian "citizen," the French commander is robbing the
Monte, and his praise of Louis' absolute rule "without constitution" illustrates
the danger, one Pound thought especially characteristic of France, of govern-
ment not based on documents.

Etruria was Napoleon's name for a new kingdom that included Tuscany. It
was ruled by his cousin, Louis I, who nearly drove it and the Monte to ruin
before he died in 1803. Louis' widow, Maria Luisa of Spain, tried to hold
Etruria for her infant son, but Napoleon divided the kingdom in 1807 and
made Tuscany a part of France. She wrote to Napoleon to protest and received
in turn a letter that Pound quotes at length to parallel the polite rape of the
Monte cash box by the French:

Madame ma soeur et
                    cousine
I have received Your Majesty's letter of
November twenty-fourth I
suppose that in the actual circumstances
She will be in a hurry to get to Spain or at least to
leave a country where she can no longer
stay with the dignity befitting her rank.   (44/226)

In this document, which Pound got from a footnote in Mengozzi, French hypocrisy reveals itself, coolly insulting Napoleon's "sister and cousin" by "mixing the pronouns / You, She"—a sure sign that it came from the general's secretary (44/227).

The final document that Pound takes from *Il Monte* is a diary by Francesco Bandini that again shows the French hypocrisy. Napoleon replaced Maria Luisa with his own sister Elisa, whom he made grand duchess of Tuscany. Upon her regal entrance into Siena, there was a grand parade where, in an apparently spontaneous outburst of "bestial enthusiasm," some young men unyoked her horses and pulled the duchess' cart themselves. Bandini wryly notes, however, that the men were "paid by the prefect / and beforehand prepared" (44/227)— an ironic contrast to the parade for Ferdinando. The duchess' magnificent entrance was further undercut by her unceremonious exit "from Lucca" (44/227) in 1814 in the wake of her brother's defeat. All that remains of any worth from the Napoleonic occupation of Tuscany is a document—"her brother's law code," and against this single achievement, the archivist of *Il Monte dei Paschi* lists the great reforms of Pietro Leopoldo:

And before him had been Pietro Leopoldo
that wished state debt brought to an end;
that put the guilds under common tribunal;
that left names only as vestige of feudal chain;
that lightened mortmain that princes and church be under tax
as were others; that ended the gaolings for debt;
that said thou shalt not sell public offices;
that suppressed so many *gabelle*;
that freed the printers of surveillance
          and wiped out the crime of lèse majesty;
that abolished death as a penalty and all tortures in prisons
which he held were for segregation;
that split common property among tillers;
roads, trees, and the wool trade,
the silk trade, and a set price, lower, for salt;
plus another full page of such actions Habsburg Lorraine
His son the Third Ferdinando, cut taxes by half,
improved tillage in Val di Chiana, Livorno porto franco.   (44/227-28)

In their biblical cadences, these Jeffersonian reforms recall charters that established the Monte in the 1620s. One reform in particular, Pietro's freeing of the printers from surveillance, strikes against the historical black-out that, Pound believed, was frustrating his own efforts to publish news of the Monte in the twentieth century. He concludes Canto 44 with the "Introduction" to *Il Monte* by "Nicolò Piccolomini," "Provveditore" of the bank in modern times. Nicolò praises his secretary Mengozzi for collecting and editing the documents in *Il Monte* and affirms that the purpose of that archival work, like Pound's, "has been to keep bridle on usury" (44/228).

Chinese Mirrors

Near the end of *The Fifth Decad of Cantos* Pound signals his next major documentary shift with three fragments from texts that, like the Monte charters, regulate human life by the rhythms of nature rather than the unnatural cycles of usury. The first comes from Hesiod's *Works and Days*:

> Begin thy plowing
> When the Pleiades go down to their rest,
> Begin thy plowing
> 40 days are they under seabord,
> Thus do in fields by seabord
> And in valleys winding down toward the sea.
> When the cranes fly high
> think of plowing. (47/237)

Pound rhymes this ancient almanac with an excerpt from Charles Bowlker's *Art of Angling*, a nineteenth-century manual, itself recast many times:

> Blue dun; number 2 in most rivers
> for dark days, when it is cold
> A starling's wing will give you the colour
> or duck widgeon, if you take feather from under the wing
> Let the body be of blue fox fur, or a water rat's
> or grey squirrel's. Take this with a portion of mohair
> and a cock's hackle for legs.
> 12th of March to 2nd of April
> Hen pheasant's feather does for a fly,
> green tail, the wings flat on the body (51/251)

Like Hesiod's instructions for plowing, Bowlker's text transmits ancient rites that correlate human activity with natural process.[1]

Between these Mediterranean and English fragments, Pound places an Oriental manuscript book that belonged to his parents.[2] The book contained eight Chinese poems, with Japanese translations, based on paintings of scenes along the River Hsiao-Hsiang. The poems, as Pound renders them, have the same archaic feel as the regulations in Hesiod and Bowlker, and similarly portray communal life ordered by the rhythms of nature:

> Comes then snow scur on the river
> And a world is covered with jade
> Small boat floats like a lanthorn,
> The flowing water clots as with cold. And at San Yin
> they are a people of leisure.   (49/244)

Supporting this harmony are political and economic regulations so delicate that the citizens barely feel the presence of "Imperial power" (49/245). The emperor who "built" a canal "for pleasure" provides a Jeffersonian vehicle for his people that endures long after his reign: "This canal goes still to TenShi" (49/245).

These fragmentary texts, too, are canals, tributaries that transmit ancient rites; they flow into Pound's translation of the *Li Ki*, the Chinese *Book of Rites*, at the opening of *Cantos LII-LXXI*.[3] The *Li Ki* draws together the Monte charters, the Leopoldine decrees, and the ritualistic fragments from Hesiod and Bowlker, by proscribing such organic regulations as the rites and duties of government officials for each month:

> The lake warden to gather rushes
>   to take grain for the *manes*
> to take grain for the beasts you will sacrifice
> to the Lords of the Mountains
>   To the Lords of great rivers
> Inspector of dye-works, inspector of colour and broideries
> see that the white, black, green be in order
> let no false colour exist here   (52/259-60)

The imagery of ceremonial harvests and sacrificial oxen recalls the Sienese parades Pound witnessed in the twentieth century, testaments to the enduring documents that wed communities to the processes of nature.

From the rites of the *Li Ki* Pound turns to another Chinese document, the *Tzu Chih T'ung-Ch'ien*, or *Comprehensive Mirror for the Aid of Government*.[4] Like the *Li Ki*, the *Mirror* grew out of a rag-bag of old historical records compiled, edited, and "made new" in 1084 A.D. by a Sung dynasty scholar named Ssu-Ma Kuang. Kuang intended his collection as a practical application of history to current government practice, and the *Mirror* became a popular history that was revised and updated numerous times by later generations. One of its major metamorphoses occurred in the twelfth century under another great scholar, Chu Hsi, who condensed and revised the *Mirror* into what John Nolde describes as a "handbook for statesmen, a didactic treatise which, if read carefully by princes and emperors, would teach them how to avoid the pitfalls of bad government by following the teachings of the Confucianists and the examples of model rulers of the past"— much the same aims Pound had in making his own compilation of historical documents in *The Cantos*.[5]

Chu Hsi's adaptation of the *Mirror* was itself updated in the early eighteenth century when the great Manchu emperor, K'ang Hsi, commissioned a Mongolian translation of this great classic. From that translation, in turn, Joseph de Mailla, a Jesuit missionary living in China in the early eighteenth century, produced a French version of the *Mirror* in thirteen volumes, *Histoire Générale de la Chine*, which he hoped would not only open a channel of communication between Europe and China but inspire political reform in his own country. Yet, like so many documents in *The Cantos*, Mailla's translation encountered the historical black-out: its publication was suppressed by the Church because Mailla would not alter the ancient dates of Chinese history to conform to biblical chronology. After nearly forty years, the book was finally published in 1777 and soon became a powerful factor in Europe's understanding of China, a "necessary document," as David Gordon notes, "in the history of the transmigration of Confucianism."[6] By recasting Mailla's French into modern English, Pound makes the *Mirror* available to modern readers, who, he seriously hoped, would apply Confucian principles to twentieth-century political and economic problems.

The textual metamorphoses of the *Mirror* are so fascinating that it is hard to agree with Wendy Flory's contention that Pound's "interest lies with the content of his source and not with its compiling, its compilers, or its influence."[7] Pound's English version of Mailla's French translation reflects the historical transformations of the *Mirror*; the Chinese history recounted by the *Mirror*, in fact, can be read as a self-reflexive image of the genesis, transmission, and renewal of the *Mirror* itself. Among the Confucian morals pointed out by the *Mirror* is that, among their other virtues, good dynasties carefully preserved and put into action ancient documents, while corrupt dynasties ignored or even destroyed the sacred texts. The *Mirror* itself is a synecdoche for all precious documents, and we trace its heroic career through Chinese history as an emblem for the enduring power of vital texts to guide a culture toward the harmonious relationship with nature celebrated in its rituals.

The *Mirror* opens with the mythical beginnings of Chinese culture, and in the accounts of the earliest godlike emperors we find, alongside the evolution of agriculture and house building, the invention of record keeping by the "knotting of cords" and of writing "out of bird tracks" (53/262). The documents produced by this rudimentary technology are the roots of the great *Mirror* itself and are duly reverenced by early sages such as "Wen Wang" (53/265), the ruler of the Chou province. Imprisoned for opposing a corrupt Shang emperor, Wen Wang recast an ancient document of the emperor "Fou Hi" into the classic "Y-king or changes" (53/266), and through it managed to communicate with his followers and incite a revolution that eventually brought down the Shang dynasty.

Wen's son Wu Wang finally overthrew the last Shang emperor, and his first act as a conqueror demonstrated a reverence for documents that would characterize the new Chou dynasty:

> Wu Wang entered the city
> gave out grain till the treasures were empty
> by the Nine vases of YU   (53/266)

By revering the nine bronze vases of the Emperor Yu (ancient documents inscribed with descriptions of the nine Chinese provinces), Wu Wang affirmed his dynasty's continuity with China's past. The Chou dynasty's love of texts can be seen, too, in the will of Wu Wang's brother and counselor, "Tcheou Kong" (Chou Kung), who

> Called for his hat shaped as a mortar board
> set out the precious stones on his table
> saying this is my will and my last will
> Keep peace
> Keep the peace, care for the people.
> Ten lines, no more in his testament.   (53/267)

Echoing Niccolò d'Este of Ferrara, who urged his son Borso to "Keep the peace" (21/96), Tcheou Kong's will, in its precision and clarity, is a textual analogue for the precious stones that surround it.

The same analogy between precious documents and precious jewels appears in the coronation ceremony arranged by another great Chou counselor, Chao Kong (Shao Kung), for Wu Wang's son "Tching-ouang" (Chêng Wang):

> Chao Kong called the historians,
> laid out white and violet damask
> For the table of jewels, as when Tching-ouang received princes.
> On the table of the throne of the West
> laid out the charters
> constitutions of antient kings and two sorts of stone   (53/267)

A prince's real treasure is not his crown jewels but the documents that guide his policy, a fact demonstrated by another great counselor, "Siao-ho" (Hsiao Ho) of the Han dynasty:

> And when TSE-YNG had submitted, Siao-ho ran to the palace
> careless of treasure, and laid hold of the records,
> registers of the realm for Lord Lieou-pang
> that wd/ be first HAN   (54/275)

Siao-ho's recognition that ancient records were more valuable than the palace jewels contrasts with the foolish minister Li-ssé (Li Ssū) of the intervening "TSIN" (Ch'in) dynasty, who advised his emperor to destroy all documents except those on agriculture and medicine:

> TCHEOU lasted eight centuries and then TSIN came
> and of TSIN was CHI HOANG TI that united all China
> who referred to himself as the surplus
> or needless bit of the Empire
>   and jacked up astronomy
> and after 33 years burnt the books
>   because of fool litterati
> by counsel of Li-ssé
>   save medicine and on field works
> and HAN was after 43 years of TSIN dynasty   (54/275)

Ironically, the dynasty that sought to destroy history by burning documents is known, in Pound's history, by that act alone.

The Han dynasty renewed the traditional Chinese reverence for historical documents, and the first Han emperor, Kao, was advised by his counselors to restore the texts that were destroyed by the Tsin black-out:

> And Lou-kia was envoy to Nan-hai, with nobility,
> and wished that the *king* (the books Chu king and Chi king)
>   be restored
> to whom KAO: I conquered the empire on horseback.
> to whom Lou: Can you govern it in that manner?
> whereon Lou-kia wrote 'The New Discourse' (Sin-yu)
>   in 12 chapters, and the books were restored.
> And KAO went to Kung fu tseu's tomb out of policy   (54/276)

The *Chu King* (*Book of Historical Documents*) and the *Chi King* (*Book of Odes*), according to tradition, were compiled by Confucius himself, though, as Carroll Terrell notes, they were "probably pieced together both before and after his time."[8] Because the texts of these compendia were lost, they had to be reconstructed through the oral tradition by old scholars who had committed them to memory. Centuries later, when the house of Confucius was torn down by a jealous emperor, it was found that the great scholar had hidden copies of these documents within the walls.

The image of Kung as the great editor and compiler of the documents that uphold society emerges in this famous anecdote of his father:

> Thus of Kung or Confucius, and of 'Hillock' his father
> when he was attacking a city
> his men had passed under the drop gate
> And the warders then dropped it, so Hillock caught
> the whole weight on his shoulder, and held till his
> last man had got out.
>   Of such stock was Kungfutseu.   (53/274)

This dramatic image serves as a metaphor for Kung's equally important act of collecting, editing, and preserving precious records even as his beloved Chou dynasty crumbled.

The restoration of Kung's classics during the Han dynasty was accompanied by the creation of new documents—Lou-Kai's (Lü Chia) treatise on government, an edition of the law code, a treatise on music, and

>   record of rites
> And this was written all in red-character, countersigned by
>   the assembly
> sealed with the Imperial Seal
>   and put in the hall of the forebears
> as check on successors.   (54/277)

As in the Chou dynasty, documents were treasured like precious jewels, for only such written texts can preserve the future from the whims of a despot. One Han prince spent his gold and silver recovering and restoring ancient documents and "preferred histories," like the "*Chu King*," to "light reading" (54/278). Equally admirable was the emperor "HAN SIEUN" (Han Hsüan Ti), under whose guidance "The text of *books*" was "reëstablished" (54/280). The greatest documentary achievement of the Han dynasty, however, came under the dowager queen "Téou-Chi" (T'ou Shih) in "a.d. 175":

> Téou-Chi brought back the scholars
>   and the books were incised in stone
> 46 tablets set up at the door of the college
>   inscribed in 5 sorts of character   (54/281)

Here the great Confucian texts literally become precious stones, even as the Han dynasty slowly crumbles under the pernicious influence of "eunuchs," "taoists," and "bhuddists" (54/281-84).

In 517 A.D., however, these documentary gems were razed for that most un-Confucian of purposes—the erection of a Buddhist temple:

> And the 46 tablets that stood still there in Yo Lang
> were broken and built into Foé's temple (Foé's, that is
>   goddam bhuddists.)
> this was under Hou-chi the she empress.
> OU TI went into cloister
>   Empire rotted by hochang, the shave-heads, and
> Another boosy king died.   (54/284)

Not until the T'ang dynasty (618-907) was this historical black-out lifted, when the great emperor T'ai Tsong—who once remarked, "Kung is to China as is water to fishes" (54/285)—recovered and made new the ancient texts. T'ai was inspired by his empress, who on her death bed urged her husband to revise the law code to make it more concise and humane:

> And TAÏ in his law code cut 92 reasons for death sentence
>   and 71 for exile
>   as they had been under SOUI
> And there were halls to Confucius and Tchéou-Kong   (54/286)

After her death, it was found that the empress had condensed the histories of earlier rulers into a compact document entitled "Notes for Princesses" (54/286), designed, like all good Confucian documents, as a guide for the conduct of future rulers. Following his wife's example, T'ai left a compact treatise to guide his son:

> And the Emperor TAÏ TSONG left his son 'Notes on
>   Conduct'
> whereof the 3rd treats of selecting men for a cabinet
> whereof the 5th says that they shd/ tell him his faults
> the 7th: maintain abundance
> The 10th a charter of labour
> and the last on keepin' up kulchur   (54/287)

T'ai's document not only guides his son but spawns another good emperor, Siuen (Hsüan Tsung), who was known as "little Tai Tsong":

Ruled SIUEN with his mind on the 'Gold Mirror' of
        TAI TSONG
    Wherein is written: In time of disturbance
    make use of all men, even scoundrels.
    In time of peace reject no man who is wise.   (55/292)

T'ai's "Gold Mirror" rhymes with those ancient documents that earlier emperors treasured above jewels, and foreshadows the creation of the *Comprehensive Mirror for the Aid of Government*.

The *Comprehensive Mirror* was compiled during the Sung dynasty (960-1279) as the culmination of a great neo-Confucian revival:

    and at the 12th moon of the 17th year of this Emperor
    Ssé-ma Kouang, Fan Tsuyu and Lieou Ju offered the
    HISTORY, called
    Tsé-tchi tong kien hang mou
        on the model of *Tso kieou ming*
    and this began with the 23rd year of
    OUEÏ-LIE of TCHEOU dynasty
    and was in 294 books.   (55/298)

The three scholars who labored for twenty years on this massive document emulated the work of "Tso kieou ming" (Tso Chiu-min), a disciple of Confucius who collected, expanded, and made new the *Annals* of his master. Such filial piety among editors and scholars extends down through the centuries to include Joseph Mailla and Pound himself as workers on the *Mirror*.

The *Mirror* underwent many metamorphoses, the two most important being Chu Hsi's abridgment and recasting of it late in the Sung dynasty and the seventeenth-century Manchu translation that Mailla used as his model, textual transformations that mirror the history they recount. As the Sung dynasty waned, barbaric tribes grew powerful, and their eventual conquest of China was marked by their translation of the *Mirror* into Manchu. When the Tartars made new this document, it signaled their continuity with a tradition whose vitality lies in texts, not in men. As early as 1022 "the tartars began using books" (55/296), and when they invaded the empire a century later, a "tartar lord" who "wanted an alphabet" ordered a "written tongue for Kin tartars" (55/299). Under "Oulo of Kin" (Shih Tsung), the greatest tribal chief, "were books set / into Nutché" (55/299)—an act of documentary transmission that parallels the Tartar takeover.

While "SUNG died of taxes and gimcracks" (55/299), the Mongols declared the "Yuen" (Yüan) dynasty in 1208. With full Mongol power established in 1280, a Sung scholar, "Kin Lusiang [Chin Li-hsiang], historian and Confucian" (56/302), devoted his last years to renewing the ancient texts and writing an introduction to the *Mirror*. Meanwhile, the Mongol emperor Kublai issued a decree on language and commissioned the Tibetan lama Pasepa (Phags-pa) to anchor the hybrid tribal dialects in a written script:

> North is the cradle of mongols
> Pasepa gave them their alphabet
> 1000 words mongol, and 41 letters   (56/304)

With this verbal "software," the new dynasty cemented its hold on China. The great documentary achievement of the Yuen was a treatise on silk culture prepared under the emperor "Gin Tsong" (Jen Tsung):

> And in the 8th moon the public works and corvée department
> presented GIN TSONG a volume on mulberry culture
> by Miao Haokien where he explains in detail the
> > growing of silk worms
> > and of unwinding cocoons
> and the Emperor had this engraved with all diagrams
> > and distributed throughout all China   (56/305-6)

From such Confucian splendor, however, the Yuen, like all other dynasties, fell—according to the *Mirror*—by "losing the law of Chung Ni / (Confucius)" (56/308).

Tartar rule was interrupted for nearly 300 years by the Ming dynasty (1368-1644), whose major contribution to the Chinese archive came when Emperor Yang Lo (Yung Lo) "commanded a '*summa*' / that is that the gist of the books be corrected" (57/311)—another metamorphosis in the organic life of the *Mirror*. The Ming dynasty was overrun by Manchu Tartars, who proclaimed the Ch'ing, China's last dynasty, which ruled until 1912. Its first great emperor, "TAI TSONG" (T'ai Tsung), like his namesake, the great T'ai Tsong of the T'ang dynasty, solidified Manchu power by putting the Confucian texts into action and grafting them onto Manchu culture. "I take letters from China," said T'ai, who also "made a Berlitz, Manchu, chinese and mongul" (58/320). His successor, "CHUN TCHI" (Shun Chih), the first Manchu emperor to rule all of China, followed T'ai by writing a preface for the "CHI-KING" (59/324), because he recognized it as a socially useful document.

Pound dwells on the *Mirror*'s account of the reign of Chun's successor "KANG HI" (K'ang Hsi), who was not only a great preserver and renewer of Chinese documents but served as a Jeffersonian channel between China and Europe. K'ang commissioned both a massive dictionary and a Pound-like concordance to all literature, and opened China to the Jesuits, though he soon had to curb their influence. Working on two documentary fronts, K'ang metamorphosed ancient Chinese texts into Manchu and exchanged texts with Europe via the Jesuits:

> History translated to manchu. Set up board of translators
> Verbiest, mathematics
> Pereira professor of music, a treatise in chinese and manchu
> Gerbillon and Bouvet, done in manchu
>   revised by the emperor as to questions of style
> A digest of philosophy (manchu) and current
> Reports on the mémoires des académies
> des sciences de Paris.   (60/332)

Out of this busy documentary "Venice," where textual canals link past and present, East and West, comes yet another reincarnation of the "History" when the *Mirror* is translated into Manchu.

The translation was finally completed under K'ang's son "YONG TCHING" (Yung Chêng), who celebrated its printing with a parade:

> And they received the volumes of history
> with a pee-rade with portable cases like tabernacles
> the dynastic history with solemnity.   (61/336)

Like the Monte charters and the decrees of Ferdinand of Tuscany, this great document is honored with an expression of the very communal harmony it records and perserves. Pound's description of the volumes of the *Mirror* as "tabernacles" links it with those great stone tablets of Confucius that were erected, razed for a Buddist temple, but then recovered and renewed.

The metamorphosis of the *Mirror* puts the community back in touch with its origins in the rhythms of the natural world:

> Eleventh month 23rd day for ceremonial ploughing
>   (I take it december)
> Out by the Old Worker's Hill
> YONG ploughed half an hour
> three princes, nine presidents did their stuff
> and the peasants in gt/ mass sang the hymns
>   befitting this field work
> as writ in LI KI in the old days   (61/336)

Yong here renews the rites recorded in that ancient collection of documents, the *Li Ki*, with which Pound opened Canto 52. That return to origins, for both Pound and Yong, is mirrored by the *Mirror* itself, which here reflects its own origins as well as the organic roots of Chinese culture. At the same time, of course, the Manchu translation of the *Mirror* moves China forward, since it was Mailla's translation of it that grafted Chinese values onto Europe and helped to shape the Enlightenment world that, in turn, generated the next collection of documents in *The Cantos*—the papers of John Adams.

VIII

The Adams Papers

If there is an American dynasty with a Confucian reverence for ancient documents, it is the Adams family, and the ten-volume edition of John Adams's papers that Pound turned to for his next block of Cantos (62 through 71) testifies to that textual piety.[1] The edition arranges Adams's papers not chronologically but according to the different kinds of documents—diaries, treatises, public papers, correspondence—so that the same historical events are seen again and again, refracted kaleidoscopically through a collage of different texts. The edition, also containing John Quincy Adams's fragmentary life of his father, was edited by grandson Charles Francis Adams—revealing filial piety that characterized the greatest Chinese dynasties.

Still, even as Pound revered Adams's papers, he saw the edition, huge and expensive, as a particularly subtle illustration of the historical black-out; while the basic ideas of Stalin and Mao Tse-tung were available in cheap editions, to most Americans Adams's papers were a closed book. Pound's staggering decision to condense and "make new" these massive volumes is reflected in the way he presents Adams himself as a maker, preserver, and renewer of documents. In particular, Adams, like Pound's ancestor Charles Wadsworth, was a defender of the colonial charter: in the course of his life, he brought out its hidden powers to defend Massachusetts from the oppression of the colonial governor Hutchinson; after the Revolution he transformed the charter into the state constitution of Massachusetts and, through his defense of that document, shaped the character of the United States Constitution. Indeed, it is the charter as much as Adams himself that is the hero of these Cantos.

Early in Canto 62 Pound excerpts the same fragment of the Massachusetts charter that Charles Francis Adams used to begin his biography of his grandfather in volume I of the Adams papers:

> for the planting
> and ruling and ordering of New England
> from latitude 40° to 48°
> TO THE GOVERNOR AND THE COMPANIE   (62/341)

These sweeping powers granted by King Charles I to the Massachusetts Bay Company made the charter a time bomb that John Adams many years later would use to argue that colonial liberties were "not the grant of princes or parliament, but the conditions of original contracts."[2] The enormous powers that lay in these colonial charters, powers not foreseen by the kings who granted them, were noticed with alarm in 1740 by Colonel Blaydon, a member of the Board of Trade and Plantation.

> BE IT ENACTED / guv-nor council an' house of assembly
> (Blaydon objectin' to form ov these doggymints)   (62/342)

Blaydon was concerned about the standard preamble used to enact laws in Massachusetts, for it seemed to grant the Assembly, the elective lower house of the colonial legislature, the authority to make the laws—an authority derived from the charter. Under Blaydon's objections, the offensive phrase was purged from official "doggymints" but in 1770 the Assembly reinstated it to combat Governor Hutchinson's attempt to annul the charter altogether.

It was James Otis, Adams later recalled, who first saw that the charter was threatened by the Writs of Assistance, which allowed customs officers to "break open ships, shops, cellars and houses" (63/354) to search for smuggled goods.

> Credit Otis with a great part of my argument
> he showed illegality; toward destroying the charters   (71/419)

Although Otis lost the case against the pernicious Writs, his fiery arguments tied the colonial charters to the British constitution, which guaranteed that an Englishman's home was his castle, where "the King's writ could not enter." A young lawyer at the time, Adams took the advice of his tutor Josiah Gridley, who said, "you must conquer the INSTITUTES" (62/352), Sir Edward Coke's monumental work, and there Adams found legal documents that traced the evolution of the British constitution through the many metamorphoses of *Magna Charta*. Adams could soon argue that the colonial charters stood in that same line of documentary metamorphosis, guaranteeing the colonists all of the written rights of Englishmen in England.

Adams's first major statement of this principle came in his "Dissertation on Canon and Feudal Law," which was printed in the *Boston Gazette* in 1765 as a protest against the Stamp Act. By requiring a government stamp and fee on all warrants, deeds, wills, and other documents, the Stamp Act was an instrument of the historical black-out as well as a violation of the British constitution's provision against taxation without representation:

WHERETOWARD THE ARGUMENTS HAD BEEN
as renouncing the transactions of Runing Mede?   (66/381)

By describing *Magna Charta* as "transactions of Runing Mede," Adams characterized the British constitution as a *contract*, like the charter, between the king and his subjects whereby the latter were given full rights in return for their allegiance.

From that contractual interpretation of the charter Adams drafted legislative instructions for his native town of Braintree that authorized its Assembly representatives to protest the Stamp Act as "UNconstitutional" (66/382). Adams's instructions were printed in the *Massachusetts Gazette* and quickly adopted

> BY 40 towns, verbatim, their instrument
> to their representatives Sam Adams has taken some
>   paragraphs
> Stamp Act spread a spirit from Georgia
> to New Hampshire   (64/355-56)

The instructions of the town of Ipswich to its representatives made the same point and explicitly invoked the charter of Massachusetts to justify colonial resistance:

> Ipswich Instructions
> right to tax selves,
>   rather as allies than as subjects
> FIRST settlement not a national act
>   and not at expense of the nation
>   nor made on land of the Crown   (64/357)

The very existence of the charter, according to the "Ipswich Instructions," indicated that England had not "founded" the American colonies as a "national act" and did not own the land; free Englishmen had purchased the land privately from the Indians and then contracted with the king in a charter that guaranteed their constitutional rights as Englishmen, including the "right to tax selves" that was violated by the Stamp Act.

The constitutional arguments implicit in the Braintree and Ipswich instructions were answered by a British writer using "Pym" as a pseudonym. In an escalating paper war that ran in a London paper and then in the *Boston Gazette* in 1766, Pym argued that Parliament's authority overrode and could even abolish the colonial charter. Taking a pseudonym of his own, "Earl Clarendon," after the great constitutional historian, Adams replied "to Bill Pym in the Baastun Gazette" (66/382). In these papers, Adams observed that the controversy over the Stamp Act had made the colonists more keenly aware of their rights and of the document that insured them: "the real constitution / which is not of wind and weather" (66/382).

That awareness of the importance of a written text as the basis of government deepened when, after the repeal of Stamp Act in 1768, the new chancellor of the Exchequer, Charles Townshend, introduced an omnibus bill into Parliament placing taxes on the colonies for lead, glass, tea, and paint. John Hancock's ship, the *Liberty*, was seized for violating the new duties, and Adams was called upon to defend Hancock and to draft legislative instructions to protest the seizure. In both capacities, Adams argued that the Townshend Acts were unjust because they had been passed "by an authority / in the constitution of which we have no share" (66/383). When that argument was countered by the legal fiction that Hancock and all colonists were "virtually" represented in Parliament and had thus given "virtual consent" to its laws, Adams insisted upon absolute adherence to the written constitution:

> whenever
> we leave principles and clear propositions
> and wander into construction we wander into a wilderness
> a darkness wherein arbitrary power
>   set on throne of brass with a sceptre of iron...   (64/358-59)

The written text alone could fend off such despotic and whimsical exercises of power.

Adams demonstrated that principle dramatically in the courtroom when he was called upon to defend four American sailors who had killed a British officer while resisting impressment. At the trial Adams piled the defense table high with books and prominently displayed a powerful document:

> that I had imported from London the
> only complete set of British Statutes
>   then in Boston or, I think, in the whole
> of the Colonies, and in that work a statute
> whose publication they feared, an
> express prohibition of empressment
> expressly IN America which statute they intended to
>   get repealed
> and did succeed 1769 toward the end of December so doing.   (64/359)

Here was no legal fiction but a text in black and white that so shook Governor Hutchinson and the judges that they dismissed the case for fear Adams would make the document public. In his *Diary* Adams quoted the statute, and Pound requotes it in symbolic defiance of Hutchinson's historical black-out:

We mean by 6th Anne chap. xxxvii section 9
IT IS ENACTED
   no mariner
be retained on any privateer ship or vessel
in any part of America... be impressed on any ship of
Her Majesty's any time after St Valentine's day 1707
    on pain of L 20. per man   (66/383)

Flat legalese here, as in Cunizza's articles of manumission, turns eloquent in its explicit guarantee of colonial rights.

By cutting immediately from that documentary bulwark to "Small field pieces happened, said Governor Hutchinson, / to point at the door of the Court House" (66/383), Pound moves to Hutchinson's next assault upon the charter. The governor had stationed troops in Boston so that their artillery just "happened" to point ominously toward the door of the building where the legislature assembled. In the instructions he drafted for Boston's representatives, "the Hnbl James Otis and Thos Cushing Esquires / Mr Sam Adams and John Hancock Esquire," Adams saw those muzzles pointing directly at the documents that guaranteed colonial liberty:

 ;;;;.....demands yr / fortitude virtue and wisdom
 to remove anything that may appear to awe or intimidate
 late attack flagrant and formal
 on the constitution itself
 and the immunities of our charters   (66/384)

Even as John Adams was exhorting his compatriots to defend the charter, he himself undertook its defense in what Charles Francis Adams calls "the most remarkable controversy that preceded the revolution."[3]

Governor Hutchinson was trying to dismantle the charter through a parliamentary act that would place the salaries of colonial judges under the Crown rather than—as provided in the charter—under the legislature. With judges dependent on the Crown (which many of them preferred to the whimsical legislature) Hutchinson felt he could bring his truculent colony firmly under the authority of Parliament. Pound traces this clash of charter and statute through documents, beginning with the instructions of the town of Cambridge to its representatives to seek a "Constitutional / means for redress" that would defend the "charter right" from Hutchinson's assault:

 money extorted from us, appropriated to the augmentation of
 burdens upon us
  independent of grants of our commons.
  attest
   Andrew Boardman town clerk   (66/384)

These instructions, whose documentary texture Pound reproduces down to the notarization of the town clerk, were attacked in the *Massachusetts Gazette* by William Brattle, a member of the Cambridge Council, who argued that Hutchinson's plan would make judicial salaries secure and independent of politics.

Brattle challenged the patriots, and Adams in particular, to debate him in print, and Adams's rebuttal, printed in the *Boston Gazette*, laid the groundwork for a radical interpretation and a making new of the colonial charter that later helped to shape the Massachusetts and "N/Y/ state" constitutions (64/362). With his adherence to the written document, Adams refuted Brattle's contention that by English common law, judges held office for life. As evidence Adams offered a crucial document—the "letters patent" by which British kings had certified and limited the terms of judges "from Edward First's time to the present" (66/385). Quoting from the letters patent, Adams showed that a judge did not serve for life but only at the pleasure of the king:

> sic: *beneplacitu nostro.*
> Ad regis nutum duratura   (66/385)

Even the great Sir Edward Coke himself, Adams pointed out, was removed from his judicial seat "by writ of the King." Adams then underscored his point by quoting the writ: "reciting that whereas etc///...appointed to desist from..."(66/385).

Moving from these documents to the colonial charter, Adams developed what Brattle, with some justification, called a "Tory" argument—that a clause in the colonial charter provided for a metamorphosis of those letters patent in the New World:

> By another clause (in our Charter)
> that the great and general court or assembly
>   shd/ have power
> to erect judicatories courts of record
> and other courts
>   to determine pleas processes plaints actions etc/
> whereby a law (2 William III) have established etc/
> and in Edward IV this Beauchamps commission
> was, for the uncertainty, VOID
> By letters patent and under great seal
> in all shires, counties palatine and in Wales
> and any other dominions   (66/385-86)

Adams here showed that the charter gave the legislature the power to certify judges just as the king did with his letters patent; he then supported his case by quoting a law of William III requiring colonial judges to have a commission from the legislature.

From the documentary rhyme between royal patents and legislative commissions at the end of Canto 66, Pound opens Canto 67 with Adams's lyric celebration of the evolution of British legal documents from the codes of "Ina, Offa, and Aethelbert," through the "Dome Book" of King Alfred, to the codification of the "folcright" under King Edward the Confessor. In all of these documents—as well as in the later writings of legal editors, compilers, and commentators—the principle of a judge serving as "a mere deputy of the King" (67/387) remained firm. Marshaling these layers upon layers of texts against Brattle, Adams, with Confucian reverence, called them precious stones that he left to "jewelers and lapidaries to refine / to fabricate and to polish" (67/387).

Adams placed the colonial charter in this long line of British documents, but Governor Hutchinson, in a speech at the opening of the Massachusetts legislature in 1773, tried to reduce the document to a mere agreement that secured partial rights for the colonists while abroad, but guaranteed their full rights whenever they returned to England. As long as they remained in America, Hutchinson maintained, they were under the control of Parliament, which could tax them even though they had no representation. Appointed to help frame the Assembly's reply to the governor, Adams insisted that the charter was a contract between the king and the colonists, and had nothing to do with Parliament. In the charter, the king gave the colonists the power to make their own laws, provided they were not repugnant to him, and the colonists in turn pledged their allegiance to the king. Adams based his interpretation on a seventeenth-century text, *Moore's Reports*; this book was not known in the colonies, but Adams was able to borrow it from his patron, Gridley, who held the only copy. This secret textual weapon threw Hutchinson and his advisers into confusion; they shot back that the charters were feudal documents that gave power over the colonies to the Crown, taking "Crown" to mean the king not as an individual but as the representative head of a government that included Parliament as well.

Pound quotes Adams's counterresponse, with its terse demolition of Hutchinson's two points:

> If we be feudatory
> parliament has no control over us
>   We are merely
> under the monarch
> allegiance is to the king's natural person 'The Spensers'
> said Coke, hatched treason denying this
> allegiance follows natural, not politic person   (62/343)

Granting Hutchinson's point that the charter was a feudal document, Adams contended that that only made it more of a contract between king and colonists, since Parliament had little power during feudal times. To the notion that "Crown" meant the king in his political role rather than as an individual, Adams cited how such sophistry was used to justify treason by the Spenser family in Coke's time. Adams's crowning touch, however, was to use Hutchinson's own history of Massachusetts to establish the contractual nature of the charter. Unlike other European settlers (Hutchinson had boasted in his history), the English colonists did not invoke the license given by the pope to all Christian kings "to seize lands of the heathen" (62/343). The English settlers purchased their land directly from the Indians; therefore, it belonged to them and not the king. The charter, as the "Ipswich Instructions" had claimed and Hutchinson's own history had corroborated, was therefore a contract through which these free landholders exchanged their allegiance to the king for his guarantee of their full rights as Englishmen, not as "mere slaves of some other people" (62/343).

It was from these sharpening controversies that Adams was able to discover what the "Cambridge Instructions" had hoped for—a "constitutional means of redress" to the crisis over the judges' salaries:

> IMpeachment by House before Council
> said shd/ be glad if constitution cd/ carry on
>   without recourse to higher powers unwritten...
>   Says Gridley: You keep very late hours!   (64/362)

Adams's late hours had been spent developing the documentary solution: the impeachment of Chief Justice Andrew Oliver for accepting a salary from the Crown. Adams arrived at this manuever by reasoning that if the king could recall his letters patent for judges, then the legislature, to which the charter gave the same right to establish courts, could impeach the judges to whom it had granted commissions.

Such a radical interpretation of the charter moved even a judge who was sympathetic to the patriotic cause to remark to Adams, "I see you are determined to explore the constitution and bring to light all its dormant and latent powers in defense of your liberty."[4] Pound twice quotes Adams's response that he would be happy if the "constitution" could carry them safely through all of their difficulties without having recourse "to higher powers unwritten" (62/343, 64/362). Pound presents Adams's victory here as a triumph of the charter itself, brought to life, made new, and put into action:

> VOTED 92 to 8 against Oliver
>   i.e. against king's pay for the judges instead of
>   having the wigs paid by the colony
>   no jurors wd/ serve

These are the stones of foundation
J. A.'s reply to the Governor
Impeachment of Oliver
These stones we built on   (62/343)

Pound's slangy recasting of the documentary language mirrors Adams's
updating of the charter to meet new times, and the image of documents as
sacred stones echoes the Chinese Cantos, where ancient charters are valued
above precious jewels.

Although it stalled in the upper house of the legislature, the impeachment
resolution fueled the British crackdown on Boston that, in turn, led to the First
Continental Congress. Pound follows Adams's journey to Philadelphia—
another of the many odysseys in *The Cantos*—and notes that on a stopover in
New York, Adams met Ebenezer Hazard and discussed the bookseller's project
of collecting American historical documents. Adams

Advised him to publish
from Hakluyt the voyage of J. Cabot   (65/363)

His advice reflects his own *periplum* to Philadelphia, where he, like the early
explorers, would help found a new world. At the First Continental Congress,
where that world began to emerge, the colonial charters were invoked to justify
American resistance to Parliament:

tenants in capite, Galloway well aware that my arguments
tend to the independency of the colonies
bound by no laws made by Parliament
        since our ancestors came here
Bill of Rights   (65/363-64)

Although he was a delegate with Loyalist sympathies, Galloway here argued
that since the British constitution gave property owners—"tenants in capite"
—the right to representation in Parliament, the colonists, who owned their
land in the New World, were not bound by any laws of a Parliament in which
they had no representation.

Such arguments, however, were too radical for what Adams called the
"nibbling and quibbling" delegates, and he returned home only to find the
charter under attack again, this time from a skillful Tory propagandist writing
under the pseudonym of "Massachusettensis." Taking the name "Novanglus,"
Adams debated the status of the charter in a series of papers (called the
"Novanglus papers") that ran "weekly in Boston Gazette from '74 until
Lexington" (62/344). Against Massachusettensis' argument that Parliament

could rightfully tax the colonies, Adams claimed that "colonization is at common law a *casus omissus*" (66/388)—nothing in British law covered colonial governance or any other application of British law outside of the realm. He reiterated the point in the "Ipswich Instructions" that the English colonies were not founded under the pope's "fanatical" grant of heathen lands to Christian kings; rather, the English colonies were purchased from the Indians and belonged not to the Crown but to settlers, who "had right of contract" with the king through the charters. Those charters gave the colonists their rights as Englishmen, Adams said, and when his opponent abridges those rights he "now leaps over law / now over fact now over charters and contracts" (67/388-89).

To illustrate his case, Adams created another documentary rhyme between the charter and two documents designed to govern other countries outside the realm of England. The first was the *Statum Wallia*:

> Edwardus Deo Gratia Angliae
> Dom. Hib. et Dux Aquitaniae terram Walliae cum incolis suis
> in nostrae proprietatis dominium   (67/389)

In this royal edict King Edward placed Wales under the Crown but not under the British Parliament—a clear analogue for Adams's interpretation of the Massachusetts charter. The next document, the "contract called Poyning's law" (67/389), formed an inverse parallel between America and Ireland. Adams traced the history of Ireland, beginning with Henry II, who "partly to divert his subjects from the murder of Becket" created the "pretence / that the Irish had sold some English as slaves" and thus obtained from the pope a license to invade Ireland. Still, even though it was a conquered country—as America was not—Ireland was allowed to govern itself through its own parliament until 1494, when Henry VII sent a military governor, Edward Poyning, to punish Ireland for supporting the House of York during the Wars of the Roses. Under Poyning, an infamous contract was passed in the Irish Parliament that made all of its laws subject to the approval of the English privy council and all laws passed by the British Parliament valid for Ireland as well. Adams's point here is that it took just such a document, registering "consent of the Irish Nation and an act in their parliament," to place Ireland under the authority of the British Parliament.

In the absence of such a document, he argued, the American colonies owed allegiance to the king but could govern themselves through the charter, a point he reinforced with the charter that King Edgar used to claim Ireland as part of his kingdom:

EDGARDUS ANGLORUM BASILEUS
insularum oceani imperator et dominus gratiam ago
Deo omnip. qui meum imperium
sic ampliavit et explicavit super regnum patrum meorum
concessit propitia divinitatis...
Hibernia habet parliamentum   (67/389)

Here the document that put Ireland under the king also granted it an independent parliament—one that stood until Poyning's contract.

As the debate deepened, it hinged on the very texture and style of the Massachusetts charter. Massachusettensis had argued that the language of the charter implicitly placed the colonies under Parliament as part of the British Empire. Adams countered that there was no "such phrase or idea" as "British empire" in "our charter," since there was no such thing as a British empire when the charter was written. Nor was Massachusettensis correct in saying that the "Style royal" of the charter placed the colonies under the Crown, which he, like Hutchinson, interpreted as the entire British government. Quoting the opening of the charter, where Charles describes himself as king of England, Scotland, France, and Ireland, Adams tauntingly asked his opponent whether the king ruled the colonies "as king over France? Ireland? Scotland or / England?" (67/390) and, since he governed each country through a different parliament, which parliament ruled America.

Finally, Adams refuted Massachusettensis' point that the presence of the Great Seal on the charter made the colony subject to Parliament:

seals, leagues, coin are prerogative absolute
to the king without parliament   (67/390)

The Great Seal, like coinage and treaties, was the province of the king alone, not Parliament, and thus as a documentary symbol further proved Adams's contention that the charter was a contract solely between the colonists and the king. Out of these closing debates the charter's texture emerges as a physical presence to underscore Adams's crowning point—that when the colonists physically brought the charter from England to America, it freed the Massachusetts Bay Company from parliamentary jurisdiction. Adams notes that at that time "the king might have commanded them to return but he did not," thus implicitly acknowledging the charter as their basis of government.

By following the arrangement of John Adams's papers, Pound marks the coincidence of the close of the Novanglus papers "In the Boston Gazette 17th April" (67/390) with the outbreak of "Hostilities at Lexington," linking Adams's vigorous defense of the charter with the tenacity of the minutemen. With the start of the Revolution, Adams again journeyed to Philadelphia, this

time to the Second Continental Congress, where he urged a metamorphosis of
the colonial charters into state constitutions. Many delegates, wary of a full
break with England, put off that task, but some asked Adams to write down his
ideas to help their colonies frame new constitutions. Published as *Thoughts on
Government* in 1776 by "Printer John Dunlap" (67/391), Adams's treatise
parallels Jefferson's *Declaration* and

> Guided pubk mind in formation of state constitutions
> e.g. N. York and N. Carolina   (62/344)

Pound quotes a letter from Patrick Henry praising the *Thoughts* for its help in
framing the Virginia constitution, which had a "family likeness" (67/392) to
Adams's blueprint. Another letter from Patrick Henry alludes to Adams's key
role in steering the *Declaration of Independence* through the Congress. The
Virginian notes that he "put up with the Declaration for unanimity's sake,"
even though it is "not pointed as I wd/ make it" (67/391-92).

It was Henry who urged Adams to accept the task of forging a treaty with
France by replacing Silas Deane as part of the American commission of
Benjamin Franklin and Arthur Lee. Pound traces this next great *periplum*
through a document included in Adams's papers, the "Log book, Sl. Tucker":

> To Capn Sam Tucker commanding the Boston:
>   (wind high and seas very rough)
> You are to afford him every accommodation in yr/ power
> and consult him as to what port you shall endeavour to get to.
>   W. Vernon
>   J. Warren
>   Navy Board, Eastern Department   (65/368)

Captain Tucker's careful log book contrasts with an absence of public records
that Adams found when he arrived in Paris. To his outrage, there were "no
documents" recording the financial transactions of Silas Deane and the other
American commissioners:

> never was before I came here
>   a letter book
>   a minute book
>   an account book   (65/372)

For Adams, who had struggled to keep documents open, this lack of records
smacked of evil. That same Puritanical insistence on the written text
hampered Adams in the French drawing-room diplomacy in which Franklin
excelled and finally prompted him to write Congress that they could save time

and money by letting Franklin be sole commissioner. Though he offered to
return home, Adams strongly hinted that he should be given a new foreign
post—minister to Holland.

In between his French and Dutch assignments, Adams did return to
Massachusetts, where he took part in the metamorphosis of the colonial
charter that he had urged for years. Massachusetts had been trying to govern
itself by the old charter, but in 1779 a constitutional convention was called to
make new the document for an independent state. Adams, back from France
and even more dedicated to the need for written texts to guide all functions of
government, was Braintree's representative and was delegated to write the new
constitution. Quoting from the formal resolution of the convention, Pound
highlights Adams's relish at this great task of recording for his people

> Fixed laws of their own making
> equitable mode of making the laws   (67/392)

Pound also excerpts a section of the constitution that specifies a love for
literature as a civic duty:

> Duty of legislators and magistrates
>   to cherish the interest of literature...
> and principles of... good humour...
>   (Constitution of Massachusetts)   (67/392)

The official document here allows Pound to indulge his hope that the poet and
legislator could be one in their dedication to the careful preservation,
transmission, and renewal of the vital texts of a culture, from laws to lyrics.

When Adams returned to Europe to negotiate a treaty with Holland, his
experience was totally different from his French mission. Through a series of
bold documentary maneuvers—publishing his instructions to negotiate a
treaty in Dutch newspapers; generating petitions from the people to their timid
representatives; and demanding from the legislature a written, "categorical
answer" to his request for diplomatic recognition—Adams finally received the
document he wanted: "5 copies, English and Dutch side by side" of a treaty.

> VERJARING
> van den veldslag by Lexington
> Eerste Memoire dan den Heer Adams
>   INDRUK of de Hollandsche Natie
> Deputies of Holland and Zeeland   (65/376)

This clipping from a Dutch newspaper notes the coincidence of Adams's
diplomatic victory with the anniversary of the Battle of Lexington. Earlier,

Pound had underscored a similar coincidence by equating the Dutch accept-
ance of Adams's "U.S.N.A. letters of credence" with the "Birth of a Nation"
(62/346).

After the Revolution, Adams remained in Europe as ambassador to
England, yet, like Jefferson, who was ambassador to France, he greatly
influenced the Constitutional Convention that met in Philadelphia in 1787.
Just before the convention began, Adams published a treatise with the bulky
title, *Defence of the Constitutions of Government of the United States of America,
Against the Attack of M. Turgot, in His Letter to Dr. Price, Dated the Twenty-
Second Day of March, 1778.* The *Defence* was a response to the Frenchman's
criticisms of state constitutions, particularly the one Adams had written for
Massachusetts. Turgot had attacked its "slavish" imitation of the British
constitution, particularly in the balance of power among an executive branch,
a judiciary, and a bicameral legislature. Adams's defense of his document is at
once a Confucian celebration of the principle of "balance" and a defense of the
great metamorphic tradition that tied the Massachusetts constitution, through
the colonial charter, to the British constitution.

As Charles Adams observed, his grandfather's *Defence* was the last great
work about constitutions; since its publication, people were "Either content
with the U.S. constitutions / or too timid to speculate on constitutions at
large" (67/393). Like *The Cantos*, the *Defence* incorporates a wide range of
texts from Greece, France, Italy, and other places in Pound's archive. Pound is
alert to the parallel and at one point notes Adams's use of a translation of *The
Odyssey*:

> There is nothing like it in the original
> Mr Pope has conformed it to the notions
> of Englishmen and Americans   (68/395)

Adams is complaining of Pope's translation of the Phaeacian episode, which
makes Alcinoüs more of a supreme monarch to suit English taste; in Homer,
Adams points out, Alcinoüs is only one among equal princes whose shared
power reaffirms the principle of balance in government.

Such balance must be rooted in a document that specifies relations among
the branches of government, and Adams's articulation of that principle made
the *Defence* something of a best seller in America, exerting a powerful
influence on the delegates to the Constitutional Convention. The *Defence*
thus functioned as the very sort of "unwobbling pivot" it defined as the
cornerstone of government, "holding the states steady" as they framed the
federal constitution. Pound makes the emergence of this document the
climactic metamorphosis of the colonial charter as it passes through Adams's
hands.[5] As president, Adams continued to defend the documents at the heart

of his culture, a defense he defined, in his inaugural address, as the aim of education itself:

> a love of science and letters
> > a desire to encourage schools and academies
> as only means to preserve our Constitution.   (62/349)

Here again Adams provided Pound with a justification for the very sort of gathering, making new, and transmitting of documents he himself had undertaken in *The Cantos*.

Even after his presidency, Adams had to "save the Constitution" again, this time from Congressman James Hillhouse, who wanted to alter the document's close adherence to the British constitution. In England, Hillhouse pointed out, hereditary distinctions among classes were reflected in the constitutional division of power among an executive branch and a bicameral legislature. Since there were no such distinctions in American society, he argued, there was no need for such an elaborate division of power. Adams's defense took the Constitution back to its roots in the colonial charters:

> I take it Mr Hillhouse is sincere
> yet wd/ it not be more representative
> to say that every colony had a governor,
> > a council, senate and house
> none of which went by heredity?   (68/396)

In a recapitulation of the whole evolution of the Constitution from the Massachusetts charter, Adams argued that the charters linked the British and American constitutions and made new the principle of balance for the New World.

Adams's renewal of the Massachusetts charter in the state constitution was itself updated in 1820 when a constitutional convention was called to revise the document after the Missouri Compromise separated the Maine territory from Massachusetts. Adams was again elected Braintree's delegate, and the convention elected him chair—an honor the old man declined—then passed a resolution praising him for his work in "diffusing knowledge of principles" (63/351). Pound cuts from this resolution to another document:

> Honoured father
> > (signed John Quincy Adams (in full)
> > 1825 (when elected)   (63/351)

John Quincy's letter of 1825 consisted only of a salutation and signature, yet it was folded round a dramatic document—the official notice of his election to the presidency from the clerk of the House of Representatives. The letter is a touching understatement of John Quincy's filial piety, and registers an American dynasty dedicated to the preservation and renewal of its country's vital texts.

Pound closes out his documentary collage with excerpts from Adams's late correspondence, which is haunted by the specter of the historical black-out. Given the few people "who comprehend ANY / system of constitution" (70/412), it was little wonder to Adams that "Histories are annihilated or interpolated or prohibited" (71/416). At times he feared that his own correspondence was being spied on or that "no printer" would publish his letters (71/418). The most depressing black-out of documents took him back to the first great defender of the charter:

> Otis wrote on greek prosody
> > I published what he wrote on the latin
> His daughter told me he had burnt all his papers
> > in melancholia
> may be from that swat on the pow
> > From '74 dates neutrality
> I begged Otis to print it (the greek prosody)
> He said there were no greek types in America
> and if there were, were no typesetters cd/ use 'em.   (71/420)

Otis's refusal to print Greek texts recalls the end of Canto 30, where the creation of "greek fonts" by the "die-cutter" Francesco da Bologna spurred a great cultural revival. The collapse of printing into the waste of newspapers that, as Adams bitterly remarked, "now govern the world" (71/415) testifies to the dead end of both the European Renaissance and the promise of the New World. Yet Otis was wrong—there were "greek types" in America: "characters" such as John Adams, whose ten volumes of massed documents stand as a monument to his fight against the historical black-out as well as to his own fears that such a fight would be futile. For Pound, who shortly after recasting those documents would know that same black-out and feel that same despair in Pisa, Adams's example, like Charles Wadsworth's, would lend strength to his defiance:

> I surrender neither the empire nor the temples
> > plural
> nor the constitution   (74/434)

The Pisan Black-out

The relative popularity of the Pisan Cantos—people like them who like nothing else in *The Cantos*—obscures the fact that they are like nothing else in Pound's epic. Before the Pisan Cantos Pound had devoted his poem to a condensation of the papers of John Adams; after Pisa he continued his documentary mode by translating the Chinese *Shu Ching*, or *Book of Historical Documents*. Probably nothing like the Pisan Cantos would have been written if Pound had not been arrested in 1945 for his pro-Mussolini broadcasts over Rome Radio and thrown into an army prison camp, the Disciplinary Training Center (DTC), near Pisa. Although he had managed to stuff a Chinese dictionary and a pirated translation of Chinese classics into his pockets when he was arrested, he lacked the kinds of documents he had been renewing and publicizing for the past twenty years; he now saw himself as a victim of the very historical black-out he had lambasted in print and over the air.

Like John Adams in his late correspondence, Pound at Pisa reflected upon the whole process of documentary preservation and transmission. His reflections were tinged at all points with his personal fears that his lifetime of gathering, condensing, and renewing texts could well be expunged by the very forces he believed had tossed him into a cage. "If the gelatine be effaced," he asks in one of his many prison meditations, "whereon is the record?" (78/479). Desperately he wanted to believe that vital records do get preserved, if not in written or printed texts, then in memory "that has carved the trace in the mind" (76/457):

> and Rouse found they spoke of Elias
> in telling the tales of Odysseus   (74/426)

One example of such endurance came from the classical scholar W.H.D. Rouse. Rouse found that the tales of Odysseus were still preserved orally by Aegean sailors, but the sailors had transformed Odysseus's name to Elias.

Further examples came from the oral traditions of Africa and Australia, which had been catalogued by the anthropologist Leo Frobenius and his pupils. One such tale describes the aborigine god "Wanjina" (74/426), "whose mouth was removed" for talking too much—like Odysseus (who never should have told Polyphemus Cyclops his name was anything but "noman, my name is noman") and like Pound himself, whose mouth was stopped after his Rome Radio broadcasts. A pun transforms the Australian "Wanjina" to "Ouan Jin," a French transliteration of the Chinese phrase "the man with an education" (74/426), and takes Pound back to Tiresias, another "man on whom the sun had gone down," yet "Who even dead, yet hath his mind entire" (47/236).[1] Since Canto 1 Tiresias has symbolized the archive of memory, and in the Pisan Cantos Pound displays the same extraordinary power of memory as he calls up old friends, old places, and old texts, and makes them new in the hell of his prison camp.

Such a memory, Pound believed, preserves the past not just as an antiquarian exercise but as a blueprint for the visionary city that has been the dream of his epic. Drawing upon oral documents in Frobenius' *African Genesis*, Pound recounts the story of the city of Wagadu, which was conjured up by the music of Prince Gassir's lute but was destroyed and rebuilt again and again:

> 4 times was the city rebuilded, Hooo Fasa
>   Gassir, Hooo Fasa   dell' Italia tradita
> now in the mind indestructible   (74/430)

The resurrected city finds its indestructible form in the mind, and Pound rhymes Wagadu with other lost cities such as Ecbatan, "the city of Dioce whose terraces are the colour of stars" (74/425); Mt Ségur in Provence; and Mussolini's Italian republic, whose collapse is figured in the "peasant's bent shoulders" at the opening of the Pisan Cantos.[2]

The city that endures in the mind was no mere wisp of dream for Pound; it rested solidly upon the oral and written documents he incorporated into *The Cantos* and could be rebuilt whenever those texts were put into action. To preserve and transmit those documents, therefore, is tantamount to the epic task of founding and protecting the city:

> I surrender neither the empire nor the temples
>   plural
> nor the constitution nor yet the city of Dioce   (74/434)

Preserving the Constitution keeps alive the possibility that the country its creators envisioned can still be erected; "God bless the Constitution / and *save* it" (79/486), Pound prays, echoing his ancestor Charles Wadsworth, who preserved another cultural blueprint in "the Charter Oak in Connecticut" (74/447).

Such stored documents can renew a civilization centuries later, as Pound suggests when he learns from a prison-camp copy of *Time* that "Winston's out." Hoping that the new government will redeem England from the usurers, Pound recalls an old document, the 1225 reissue of *Magna Charta*:

> To watch a while from the tower
>   where dead flies lie thick over the old charter
> forgotten, oh quite forgotten
> but confirming John's first one,
> and still there if you climb over attic rafters   (80/514)

Imprisoned himself, Pound can dream of the resurrection of Mussolini's republic when one of its founding documents is recovered and made new:

> "alla" non "della" in il Programma di Verona
>   the old hand as stylist still holding its cunning
> and the water flowing away from that side of the lake
> is silent as never at Sirmio
>   under the arches
> Foresteria, Salò, Gardone
>   to dream the Republic.   (78/478)

Quoting Mussolini's guarantee of property as a right for all in the *Programma di Verona*, Pound equates the editor's cunning preservation of such sacred texts with the endurance of water and stone; as these natural forces endure, so do the dreams of England and Italy inscribed in documents like *Magna Charta* and the *Programma*.

Even the Hebrew city of Zion could be built, Pound cagily implies, if the Jews "respected at least the scrolls of the law," for in such documents as "Leviticus / chapter XIX" there are proscriptions for a just price which, if followed, could "rebuild" with "justice Zion" (74/454). Before such documents can be put into action, however, they must be transmitted, and Pound's meditations on the scriptures are interrupted by a taunting voice:

> Hey Snag wots in the bibl'?
> wot are the books ov the bible?
> Name 'em, don't bullshit ME.   (74/430)

The voice comes from a fellow prisoner at Pisa, a black American soldier who challenges Pound to perform the standard Sunday School exercise of reciting the books of the Bible from memory. Like the blacks whose documents Frobenius catalogued in *African Genesis,* this prisoner has had to preserve his culture orally, a reminder to Pound that the records of the past must ultimately reside in the archive of human memory.

One such archive is transcribed in M.E. Speare's *Pocket Book of Verse,* a collection of poetic documents Pound found "on the jo-house seat" (80/513) of the prison camp latrine. Speare's book maps the metamorphoses of Aphrodite, the figure for poetic song who emerges from the Homeric Hymns at the end of Andreas Divus's *Odyssey,* through the voices of English lyric poets; from Chaucer's

> Your eyen two wol sleye me sodenly
> I may the beauté of hem nat susteyne   (81/520)

through the "Althea" of Lovelace, another imprisoned poet, to her modern reincarnations in Symons's "Esther" and Blunt's "I Am The Torch." Yet, while Pound can celebrate the renewal of Aphrodite in these songs, he laments the "loss of the fly-by-night periodicals / and our knowledge of Hovey, / Stickney, Loring" (80/495). Lost, too, are "the texts" of Sadakichi Hartmann's "early stuff," and Pound ponders the historical black-out in one of its subtlest forms as he rummages through Speare's *Pocket Book:* "and wd/ Whitcomb Riley be still found in a highbrow anthology" (80/510).

Nearly lost was Edward FitzGerald's lyrical translation of *The Rubáiyát of Omar Khayyám.* Pound recalls how it was published but unread, unknown, relegated to the bookstore junk heaps and "lay there till Rossetti found it remaindered / at about two pence" (80/510). The lucky plucking-out of the book from oblivion has its analogue in Pound's tale of how a drowning Swinburne was hauled out of the sea by Greek fishermen, for whom he recited Aeschylus out of the vast storehouse of his memory. The spouting Swinburne is metamorphosed in Pound's recollection of Yeats composing in Stone Cottage, making "The Peacock" out of a "mouthful of air":

> I recalled the noise in the chimney
> as it were the wind in the chimney
>   but was in reality Uncle William
> downstairs composing
> that had made a great Peeeeacock
>   in the proide ov his oiye
>   had made a great peeeeeeecock in the...
> made a great peacock
>   in the proide of his oyyee   (83/533-34)

Yeats's creation, with its erotic and scatalogical inflections, rivals God's power to create the peacock and everything else by speaking. Like the memorable and quotable *Rubáiyát*, Yeats's written verse vibrates with the sound of the human voice, "in-spires," and carves its trace in the mind.

Playing off Yeats's remark at the opening of Canto 83—"Nothing affects these people / Except our conversation" (83/528)—Pound introduces another Irishman, the medieval philosopher Johannes Scotus Erigena, and celebrates conversation, the oral source of prose as song is of poetry:

> wrote the prete in his edition of Scotus:
> Hilaritas   the virtue *hilaritas*
>
> the queen stitched King Carolus' shirts or whatever
> while Erigena put greek tags in his excellent verses   (83/528)

Erigena was one of the last western Europeans to speak Greek, renewing the classical world in conversation with the same care as that with which he wove classical allusions into the poems he wrote for King Charles the Bald of France. According to the nineteenth-century "prete" who collected and edited Erigena's *De Divisione Naturae*, however, it was Erigena's conversation, with its "hilaritas"—its lively wit—that engaged the king and, Pound believed, inspired the troubadours. For that inspiration, presumably, Erigena's bones were dug up and scattered during the Albigensian Crusade.[3]

However, even that particularly gruesome instance of the historical black-out could not silence Erigena's voice and the classical past it carried; through "Gemisto" (83/528) Plethon's conversations and lectures, Greek culture was revived in western Europe. When one of the listeners, Sigismundo Malatesta, dug up Plethon's remains in Greece and brought them back for burial in the Tempio at Rimini, he undid the desecration of Erigena's grave. Even Erigena's habit of weaving Greek tags in his verses was reincarnated in Malatesta's court poet: "Basinio's manuscript with the / greek moulds in the margin" (82/524). At Pisa, Pound's renewed belief in conversation as a means of preserving and transmitting the past moved him to converse in imagination with old friends, stressing the subtlest nuances of their voices—Santayana, who "kept to the end of his life that faint *thethear* / of the Spaniard" (81/519); Mussolini, whose accent was marked by the "*v* for *u* of Romagna" (81/519); and Senator Edwards, who "cd/ speak / and have his tropes stay in the memory 40 years" (83/536). The most memorable voice that came to Pound in prison, however, was from the "conversation" of Ford Madox Ford, "consisting in *res* non *verba*" and manifesting a "humanitas" (82/525) that rhymes with the "hilaritas" of Erigena's talk.

Interwoven with the textures of voices Pound hears in Pisa are his speculations on the nature of writing, speculations occasioned by the dearth of written material in prison and the difficulty of doing any writing of his own. Those difficulties were eased by a kindly black soldier who made a writing table from army crates and gave it to Pound with the Odyssean advice, "Doan you tell no one" (74/434) who made it. As he writes, Pound searches for a script that will embody the human voice and incorporate, like Ford's conversation, the "thing" and not the "word." Gazing at birds on the barbed wire fence of the prison, Pound wonders if musical notation began when someone saw birds perched on parallel lines: "2 on 2" and "6 on 3, swallow-tails" (79/487):[4]

> f   f
>   d
>
>   g
>   write the birds in their treble scale   (85/525)

From the natural sight of birds on wires came musical notation, then the poetic line, the a-a-x-a rhyme scheme of FitzGerald's *Rubáiyát:*

    4 birds on 3 wires, one bird on one   (79/485)

In Canto 76 Pound underscores the parallel between musical and poetic writing by transcribing Jannequin's Bird Canzone, a song rooted in the troubadours and the "Persian hunting scene"[5] of the *Rubáiyát.*

On the crates of his writing table, Pound found an example of the oldest form of writing, the seal:

> (O Mercury god of thieves, your caduceus
> is now used by the american army
>   as witness this packing case)   (77/471)

In view of Mercury's dual role as god of healing and of thievery, the medical insignia indicts both the army and Pound himself, as recipient of a "scrounged" writing table. Yet the curative powers of that caduceus emerge when we recall that in Canto 1 Mercury's wand was a golden bough that could lead one through hell.

Another classical emblem is the "seal Sitalkas" (74/437), which Allen Upward used in place of his name on the title page of his books.[6] Appropriately enough for a "man with no name," the seal shows a man with a winnowing fan on his shoulder, recalling Odysseus, who at the end of *The Odyssey* is instructed to journey inland with an oar on his shoulder until someone asks him if it is a winnowing fan—a sign that he is so far inland that people do not know of the sea. As he remembers Upward's theory that the sacrificial victim is a central symbol in all cultures, Pound reads his own image, as well as Upward's, in the seal. Like Malatesta, Upward had helped to preserve the ancient world as both scholar and soldier—translating Eastern and classical texts and running the blockade of Crete after World War I. In Africa he, like Frobenius, conversed with African tribes in the oldest of languages—signs—and once stood off a hostile tribe "by Niger with pistol" (77/437). Back in England, Upward struck the same stance, trying to combat the barbarism of British culture "with a printing press by the Thomas bank" (74/437), but, like James Otis, he gave up trying to revive the modern world by translating and printing ancient documents. In total identification with the figure of the victim on his "seal Sitalkas," Upward finally "shot himself."

Although the seal prefigures Upward's fate, it also testifies to the endurance of the past in such records as the seal medals cast by Matteo di Pasti and Pisanello:

> for praise of intaglios
> Matteo and Pisanello out of Babylon
> they are left us
> for roll or plain impact
> or cut square in the jade block   (74/437)

For Pound, the beautiful medals of Sigismundo and Isotta embody the renewed classicism of Malatesta's age. In further contrast to Upward's despair, Pound recollects a conversation with T.E. Lawrence who "wd/ not talk of" England's betrayal of the Arabs but "wanted to start a press / and print the greek classics" (74/444).

The power of individuals and cultural traditions to endure despite the historical black-out finds its fullest expression in Chinese culture. It was in China, Pound recalls, that scholars reconstructed from memory the destroyed Confucian classics, and there, too, "jade block" seals, like those that Matteo and Pisanello inscribed, were used for printing. Chinese script, moreover, is a textual equivalent of Ford's conversation that united word with thing, and Pound celebrates its organic power, which can emerge even from such a debased form of printing as a slick magazine. After reading an article in *Time* about the empress dowager of China, Pound muses,

> I wonder what Tsu Tsze's calligraphy looked like
> they say she could draw down birds from the trees   (80/495)

Here the image of Chinese writing circles back to Pound's celebration of the birth of musical notation from birds on wires, a figure for writing that can resist the historical black-out.

This fascination with Chinese writing deepened after Pound was removed from the Pisan prison camp and returned to America to stand trial for treason. In a still notorious case, he was found mentally incompetent and committed to St. Elizabeths Hospital. In that asylum he wrote the *Rock-Drill* Cantos—a title taken from Jacob Epstein's sculpture of a human figure mounted aggressively and erotically upon a jackhammer. These Cantos open with the thick black *Ling* ideogram and continue Pound's deep burrowing into the documents of the past with a redaction of one of the oldest Chinese documents, the *Shu Ching*.[7] Like so many of Pound's secondhand sources, the *Shu* is a rag-bag of speeches, conversations, and proclamations drawn largely from four ancient dynasties—the Yu, the Hia, the Shang, and the Chou. By tradition, its compilation is attributed to Confucius who, a rock-driller himself, dug into ancient documents, probing, condensing, and renewing district and family records in the hope that the past could redirect the disoriented age in which he lived.

In *The Fifth Decad of Cantos* Pound had described the burning of the *Shu* in 213 B.C. and its patient reconstruction by old scholars who had committed portions of the work to memory, one of whom reportedly could recite the entire *Shu* by heart. After his own experience at Pisa, Pound could again celebrate this victory of memory and voice over the historical black-out, and *Rock-Drill* opens with the clash between preservers and destroyers of documents—Cleopatra, who "wrote of the currency," and "Queen Bess," who "translated Ovid," set against those who "index'd" Galileo and "scatter old records" (85/543). Like the shade Tiresias, such "shadows" preserve the vital records of the past, an enterprise symbolized by the "hsien form"—an ideogram depicting a bamboo slip binding documents together.

Confucius himself was one of those shades, and not only did he bind the documents of the *Shu* together, but he shrewdly preserved a copy in the walls of his house. In 140 B.C., after the oral reconstruction of the *Shu* was completed, the original manuscript was found, and the version we now have is a conflation of these oral and written layers. Pound, in turn, digs into this document through a many-layered translation by a French Jesuit, Sephraim Couvreur. On every page of Couvreur's edition are found the linguistic strata of original Chinese ideograms, their French transliterations, and then, in parallel columns, Couvreur's Latin and French translations. Through all these layers—as well as in a Chinese dictionary and in James Legge's English translation, with its copious notes on the roots and shades of meaning of each ideogram—Pound tries to get back to the original voices in the *Shu*.

The *Ling* ideogram that opens Canto 85 means "sensibility" and is used by the first Shang emperor, T'ang, and his minister, I Yin, to justify their overthrow of the corrupt Hia dynasty in 1766 B.C.: "Our dynasty came in," they argue, "because of a great sensibility" (85/543). Their argument rests upon an ancient Chinese doctrine, the Mandate of Heaven or Celestial Decree, which became the basis of the Chinese constitution. Like *Magna*

Charta, the Mandate of Heaven balances the power of the government with the rights of the people, stipulating that "the ruler rules the people for the people's good."[8] When a ruler violates the Mandate of Heaven, the people have the right to overthrow him, and in the *Shu Ching* the Mandate is first invoked in "The Announcement of T'ang" and "The Instructions of I," two formal speeches from the section devoted to the Shang dynasty.

From ideograms in these two documents Pound draws metaphors that define the organic nature of the Mandate of Heaven. "The Announcement of T'ang" argues that a good ruler ought to establish an order as natural "as the grass and tree" (85/544), and in its early years the Hia dynasty, according to "The Instruction of I," provided such order:

> "Birds and terrapin lived under Hia,
>   beast and fish held their order,
> Neither flood nor flame falling in excess"   (85/545)

But Hia degenerated until its last emperor became a mere figurehead,

> This "leader", gouged pumpkin
>   that they hoist on a pole   (85/545)

Thus, the Hia lost the Mandate of Heaven and was justly overthrown by T'ang, who founded the Shang dynasty and perpetuated the organic sensibility manifested in the *Ling* ideogram.

After T'ang's death, the old counselor I Yin tried to transmit this sensibility to T'ang's son, Tai-Tsung, but at first the young emperor refused to listen. In his "Instruction" I Yin states, in Pound's slangy American, that he will not "pamper this squirrel-headedness" that could "bitch this whole generation in fish-traps" (85/546). Pound gets his homespun image of "fish-traps" from the ideogram for "deception," which resembles the cross-hatchings of a snare. I Yin finally sent Tai-Tsung to his father's tomb "to think things over," and Pound renders the happy outcome of I Yin's corrections through Couvreur's transliteration of the ideograms meaning "the young king came to virtue in the end":

> k'o
> tchoung
> iun
> te   (85/546)

Cutting to Couvreur's Latin translation, Pound notes that I Yin then restored the government to the emperor—"reddidit gubernium imperatori"

(85/547)—then frames his multilingual quarryings from the *Shu* with Couvreur's French: "Justice, d'urbanité, de prudence" (85/544). Couvreur's phrase, echoing the slogan of the French Revolution, embodies the Mandate of Heaven, and Pound thumps another parallel home by waving section "III. 6. xi" of the *Shu* and declaring, "Right here is the Bill of Rights" (85/547).

Like the Bill of Rights, the Mandate is a "pivot" (85/547) that balances the power of the emperor with the rights of the people. In the *Shu* that balance is reflected in the dialectical structure of documents where the emperor's voice is balanced by a counselor who speaks for the rights of the people. In one of these dialogues, "The Charge to Yueh," the emperor "KAO TSOUNG," 1324-1265 B.C., addresses his minister, Yueh:

> Whetstone whirling to grind,   jòu
>
>   tso
>
>   li
>
>   cymba et remis
>
> Trees prop up clouds   (85/549)

Here, drawing on all the linguistic layers of Couvreur's edition of the *Shu*, Pound renders the emperor's plea for balance from his counselor. In the transliterated Chinese, Kao compares himself to a steel weapon and asks Yueh to be his whetstone; in Latin, he calls himself a boat ("cymba") and asks the counselor to be his oars ("remis"); finally, in Pound's English translation of the rain ideogram, a cloud over two trees, Kao compares himself to parched land and asks Yueh to be the fruitful rain. Pound's imagistic translations also capture the oral texture of the *Shu*, as when he renders the ideogram for anger by having Yueh caution the emperor not to be "flame-headed" (85/550). By elaborating the *Hsien* ideogram, a head with sun beams running through it like silk threads, Pound can have Kao gratefully reply, "Up to then, I just hadn't caught on" (85/550).

Just as the Mandate of Heaven was used by the Shang dynasty to overthrow the Hia, it was ultimately invoked against a late Shang emperor who had lost sight of the people's rights. The succeeding dynasty, the Chou, was established by Wu Wang and his army of "Gentlemen from the West" (85/552), and Pound translates Wu Wang's "Great Declaration," which makes new the Mandate of Heaven and the *Ling* ideogram: "Our dynasty came in because of a great sensibility" (85/551). The next document Pound takes from the *Shu*, the "Announcement of the Duke of Shao," contains, according to Lin Yutang, "The clearest exposition of the 'mandate of Heaven.' "[9] The Duke of Shao was Wu Wang's minister, and in his "Announcemnent" he informs the emperor's successor, Ch'eng, that his new capital city has been completed. The ideograms 土 (earth) and 中 (pivot) (85/554) place the capital at the center of the world, the incarnation of the social pivot expressed in the Mandate and reincarnated in such leaders as John Adams, whose motto, "I am for balance" (70/413), shaped the American Constitution's balance of power.

Another human embodiment of that principle is the Duke of Chou, Ch'eng's next prime minister, whose speech to the officers of the defeated Shang dynasty is another metamorphosis of the Mandate of Heaven. The duke compares Wu Wang's revolution against the Shang dynasty to "Tch'eng T'ang," the first Shang emperor, who "overthrew Hia" (85/555). Again, Pound traces the Mandate's evolution from ideograms, through Couvreur's Latin ("Praestantissimos regere"—the most outstanding men should rule), and finally into French, as the duke appeals to the recalcitrant soldiers, "O nombreux officiers," to become citizens of the new dynasty (85/555,556). At the heart of the duke's address, once again, is the *Ling* ideogram: "Our Dynasty came in because of great Ling" (85/555).

In order to guide the young emperor Ch'eng, the Duke of Chou compiled a document that mirrors the *Shu Ching* itself—a gathering of records from the great emperors of the past. The duke's act of preserving, condensing, and making new these documents inspired Confucius to compile the *Shu*, and Pound follows these ancient Chinese editors by updating their texts for his own age, particularly when their records reflect sound economic policies, like those of Wu Wang, who never taxed the people "above just contribution" (85/557). The next document that Pound renews emphasizes the role of good counselors in preserving the balance of power mandated by heaven. Addressing a fellow minister who was threatening to retire, the Duke of Chou urged his colleague to stay on and help to advise the emperor because, as Pound voices it, "We flop if we cannot maintain the awareness" (85/557). That awareness is the sensibility manifested in the *Ling* ideogram, a sensibility maintained not only by kings and counselors but by scholars, like Chou and Confucius and Couvreur, who preserve and transmit vital texts. Corrupt dynastic emperors, however, "Cdn't see" that the "ming" (decree of God) was "in some fine way tied up with the people" (85/558). In the roots of the *Touan* ideogram (which he identifies with "The Ta Seu," or Great Charter), Pound sees an ax and documents bound up in silk, an emblem of the condensing and preserving of ancient records.

Ling resurfaces in the Duke of Chou's appeal to the Mandate of Heaven in his address to the defeated Shang officers. The Shang "Lost the feel of the people" (86/560), says Chou, and Pound highlights the duke's constitutional argument with the *Tien* (document), *Chiao* (teach), and *Chien* (bamboo slip for documents) ideograms (86/560-61). After the death of this great duke, the new emperor, W'ang, summons his ministers and asks them a question that goes right to the heart of Pound's enterprise in *The Cantos:* "Quis erudiet without documenta?" (86/561)—How will you teach without documents? In accord with Confucian principles, W'ang urges the ministers to follow the duke's example by putting the ancient documents ("touan") into practice ("jóung") and by making their own documents ("Edictorum") full ("t'i") and concise ("iao").

The documentary metamorphoses of the Mandate of Heaven culminate in 950 B.C., in the reign of the great Chou emperor "MOU WANG" (86/562) when a written constitution is drawn up. In a conversation between "King Mou" and his minister—another of those symbolic dialogues in the *Shu Ching* where a counselor balances an emperor's power with the rights of the people—Mou pleads with his minister to "Live up to your line / and the constitution" (86/562). Pound quotes a section of the new constitution, one that instructs judges to examine the appearance of each case ("etiam habitus inspiciendus"). Couvreur's Latin here creates a rhyme with Western law, and Pound elaborates his linguistic analogies by placing the ideogram for *constitution* beside the English word *constitution.* Because that ideogram looks so much like the initial *Ling* ideogram, the two figures symbolize the long process by which the ancient Mandate of Heaven, emblematized by *Ling,* has metamorphosed into a written constitution.

A Memorial to Archivists
and Librarians

From his cell at St. Elizabeths Hospital, Pound launched another documentary *periplum* through *Rock-Drill* and *Thrones*, one that carried him back to his favorite places—early nineteenth-century America, the Mediterranean world, and China. In a wide range of texts he found men and women, like himself, who had preserved documents against the historical black-out, and here Pound celebrates and renews their struggle in a poetic "memorial to archivists and librarians" (96/654).[1] In the memoirs of Missouri Senator Thomas Hart Benton, *A Thirty Year's View: The History of the Workings of the American Government from 1820 to 1850*, he found an American counterpart to the *Shu Ching*, a record of important speeches and conversations among good rulers and counselors. In his preface Benton described his book as a "weaving" of extracts from these speeches around a narrative account of his career, a documentary technique much like Pound's in *The Cantos*; like Pound, he hoped his archive would preserve history accurately for future generations. He described himself as a man who has "spoken history . . . acted history . . . lived history," an adviser to presidents, like the great counselors of the *Shu Ching*, whose "most familiar conversation" was history itself.[2] Yet Benton's voice had been silenced, Pound believed, by the forces of usury, and in Canto 88 we see that struggle reflected in Benton's account of his battle against the charter of the National Bank.

From the twenty-sixth chapter of *A Thirty Year's View*, Pound takes Benton's account of a duel in 1826 between Henry Clay, then secretary of state, and Senator John Randolph of Virginia. The duel had started over a document—a letter from the Mexican ambassador Salazaar inviting the United States to a conference of Latin American nations in Panama. The United States had originally been excluded from the conference, which was organized by Simon Bolivar, and Randolph believed that the document had been " 'forged or manufactured' " (88/577) by Clay and President John Quincy Adams to gain public support for American interference in Latin American affairs. Randolph made his accusation on the Senate floor and "declined to offer / explanation" for his suspicions beyond noting a "strong likeness / 'in points of style' to other papers" by Clay. When Clay challenged Randolph to a duel, the Virginian first insisted upon his constitutional right as a senator to make such accusations, then gallantly waived his immunity to accept Clay's challenge.

Benton recounts his visits to both men before the duel. At Randolph's home, he learns that the senator plans to fire into the air instead of shoot at Clay. Pound, however, skips the duel and focuses upon the comic episode of Randolph making out his will. Randolph sends his servant "Johnny to Branch bank" for gold, but when the servant returns to say that the bank is out of gold, Randolph goes there himself, refuses to accept bank notes, and succeeds in withdrawing all of his "MONEY" in gold (88/579). Pound thus depicts Randolph as a swashbuckling battler of illicit documents—from diplomatic correspondence to bank notes—and prepares for Benton's war against the charter of the National Bank.

Pound links that charter with the equally pernicious charter of the Bank of England. Quoting his pet phrase from William Paterson's "1694" prospectus granting the Bank of England interest "on what it creates out of nothing" (88/579), Pound makes the American document a metamorphosis of Paterson's usurious license. With the election of Andrew Jackson, the battle against renewing that charter opened, and Thomas Hart Benton led the fight on the Senate floor. Even though the charter would not come up for renewal until 1836, Benton launched an attack in 1831 against the bank's "unconstitutional fraud" (88/582) of excluding all foreign coins except "Spanish milled dollars" from circulation. He saw this exclusion as a plot to impose the bank's own paper currency on the nation, particularly on the western farmers who lived far from American mints and depended upon the free flow of foreign coins:

> A currency of intrinsic value FOR WHICH
> They paid interest to NOBODY   (88/582-83)

This ruse to force the nation to accept its "unconvertable paper" notes, even as America's mines were "yielding" a profusion of metal, was a bank strategy designed by its director, "Geryon's prize pup, Nicholas Biddle" (88/583). Like John Randolph demanding "real" money from his local teller, Benton argued for a "currency of hard money" and denounced the chicanery of the Senate Finance Committee in presenting a favorable report on the bank so late in the session that the document was "laid on the table" (88/585) without debate. The report was then "printed" and circulated in bank-controlled newspapers to garner support for renewing the charter.

Benton's call for hard cash from the nation's mines reminds Pound of the great Chinese emperor "T'ang," who understood the "distributive function of money" and "opened the copper mine" (88/580). The principle of tapping the organic wealth of the land, that principle upon which the Monte dei Paschi was chartered, is hammered out again in Benton's speech urging a tariff on imported indigo to rekindle what had once been a vital American industry. After Great Britain began to import its indigo from India, the American industry, centered in the southern states, so dwindled that by 1814, Benton complained, our "manufacturers seek it, now seek it, abroad / and pay ready money" (88/583) for it to British importers. To illustrate the need to encourage native industry, Benton read a document aloud on the Senate floor, a Persian proclamation of 1823 offering land to emigrants "for production of barley, rice, cotton / free of any tax or of any contribution whatsodam" (88/584). Benton's own reverence for the land as the basis of economic values is reflected in his praise of Nathaniel Macon, who, like the great Chinese emperors, "Used plow and hoe until he was sixty" (88/584) as a ritualistic expression of the roots of his political ideals and actions.

Even though he failed to bring the charter up for debate before its scheduled renewal, Benton's speech started the institution "on its downhill course,"[3] and Pound marks that crucial point with a citation that we can look up:

page 446
column two

("Thirty Years", Benton)   (88/583)

Even as Benton spoke, the historical black-out struck—pro-bank senators charged that his comments were out of order, but "The Vice President directed that Mr Benton proceed" (88/586). Renewing the charter, Benton argued, would make an institution already "too great and too powerful" even more "prodigious," since the charter allowed the bank "boundless emissions" of paper notes and placed that power in a company of private individuals, many of them foreigners living "in a remote corner" of the world (88/586). That company, moreover, was run by a seven-man board of directors—none of whom was elected by the people.

As Benton enumerates these points in the charter, the document emerges as a license for "monopoly absolute," like that of the Bank of England, and Benton underscores the parallel by quoting a letter from the "Court of Directors" of the Bank of England to William Pitt, telling the prime minister flatly that the British government could borrow no more money. Such a letter, coming in the crucial year 1795, threw Britain into economic chaos in an awesome illustration of "Political as well as pecuniary" power that can "subjugate government" (88/586). Benton also notes that when it was founded in 1694, the bank lent the British government "One million 200,000" pounds, with an interest charge of "80,000" pounds and expenses of "4" thousand (88/587). Since then, the British national debt has risen to "900 Million" pounds, with comparable increases in interest and expenses. Out of the "GERM, nucleus" of that original charter, according to Benton, the Bank of England has nourished the cancer of public debt, and renewal of the charter of the National Bank would "beget and prolong useless wars; / aggravate inequalities; make and break fortunes" (88/587).

Pound records the vote on Benton's motion to open debate on renewal of the charter:

> Yeas:
> Barnard, Benton, to 20.
> Nays: 23 Webster, Wil-
> ley
> (88/587)

Although the bank's supporters, led by Webster, narrowly defeated the resolution, Benton's speech was circulated—as Pound circulates it again here in *The Cantos*—and helped to sway public opinion against the charter. Benton continued the fight in 1832 by speaking out against the bank's "illegal and vicious paper" currency, issued through small regional banks but redeemable for gold and silver only at "Philadelphy" (88/587). Another metamorphosis of Randolph's comic struggle with his bank teller, this ploy forced "labouring people," who could not travel to Philadelphia to redeem them, to use the notes as "local currency" until "through 'wear and tear'" they were never returned and thus "became a large item of gain / (for the Bank)" (88/588). Asking for a "joint" resolution "against these orders as / currency," Benton attacked them as undocumented documents:

> Are they signed by the president?
> They are not.
> Are they under the corporate seal?
> Are they drawn in the name of the body?   (88/588)

Benton here sounds like a backwoods preacher, but still he failed to muster the votes to open debate on renewing the bank's charter.

Pound concludes Canto 88 with one more assault on that document and the conspiracy of silence that protected it. The bank's supporters wanted to whisk the charter's renewal through the House of Representatives and the Senate without debate, but Benton was determined "to force the bank into defences which would engage it in general combat and lay it open to side-blows as well as direct attacks."[4] One such side-blow involved him in some documentary juggling of his own. If he could persuade the House to open an investigation of the bank just as the Senate was about to consider renewal of the charter, the bank would be squeezed from both sides: if it tried to stop the investigation, it would show it had something to hide; if the investigation took place, the bank's corruption would be exposed. Seeking out a new congressman, "Mr Clayton" of Georgia, Benton urged him to introduce a House resolution calling for an investigation of the bank by a select committee. To back the resolution, Benton gave Clayton a secret document of his own:

> And as for the charter?
>> Seven violations,
>> 15 abuses."
> These Mr Clayton read to the house, not Polk,
>> Mr Clayton,
> from a narrow strip of paper, rolled round his finger
> so that the writing shd not be seen,
>> He not having had leisure to copy and amplify.   (88/588-89)

On this tiny piece of paper Benton gave Clayton a list of the bank's violations and abuses of its charter, and on the House floor, Clayton read the list aloud but concealed it so that no one could see Benton's handwriting. This closing image reflects Pound's own enfolding and recasting of Benton's words, giving them new blood, circulating them in the never-ending fight against usury. The inverted spade at the close of the Canto is an image of digging into the past—the bank investigation Clayton calls for from the House floor as well as Pound's own delving into historical documents throughout *Rock-Drill*.

From the America of Benton and Jackson, the next documents that Pound recasts take him back to the classical world where his poem began, and one of the texts, *The Life of Apollonius of Tyana*, specifically recalls Odysseus' meeting with Tiresias.[5] Apollonius was a second-century philosopher whose wanderings, like those of Odysseus, took him to Asia and Africa, and ranged from the grimly realistic to the utterly fantastic. As always, Pound's interest lies as much with the story of the text as with the stories within the text, and the *Life* is a document that resembles many others in *The Cantos*. Although Apollonius wrote nothing himself, his disciples preserved his life in fragmentary memoirs and histories, and in 217 A.D., about 100 years after his death, Roman Empress Julia, wife of Septimius Severus, commissioned a Greek sophist named Philostratus to edit and improve the style of these scattered accounts:

> Daughter of a sun priest in Babylon
>> told Philostratus to set down this record
>>> of TYana   (94/639)

Philostratus undertook the project to defend Apollonius from attacks by the early Christian Church, which regarded him as a dangerous rival to Christ and a promulgator of pagan rites.

Pound obviously felt a kinship with Apollonius, one deepened by Apollonius' reputed knowledge of all languages—even that of the animals—and his imprisonment for sedition by Emperor Domitian. Thus, Pound was disturbed by the nearly complete success of the black-out of the *Life of Apollonius*, which was not translated into English until 1811:

> no full trans/ till 1811,
> remarks F. C. Conybeare, the prelector,
> who says it is (sic:) "lightly written"
> although no theologian touches it . . . well?
> NO! (94/637)

Pound is quoting from the introduction to the second English translation of the *Life* as by F.C. Conybeare, who also provided the original Greek in the sort of multilayered text that allowed Pound to weave back and forth among languages and cultures. Just as he plays with Conybeare's translations of particular words, Pound challenges the Oxford don's characterization of the *Life* as "lightly written," implying that Christian theologians have had to steer clear of its explosive paganism.

In *The Cantos* Pound continues the work of Philostratus and Conybeare by making new the *Life* and integrating it with the other documents he has incorporated into *The Cantos*. By emphasizing Apollonius' conversations with various rulers he encountered in his wanderings, for example, Pound can splice the *Life* with the *Shu Ching*:

> and Apollonius said to King Huey

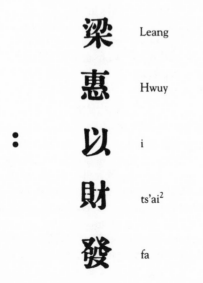

Leang

Hwuy

i

ts'ai²

fa

wu[2]

i[3]

pao[3]

rhymed in Taxila

Phraotes' tigers worship the sun.

(94/636)

In Taxila, Apollonius, like a Chinese counselor, advised King Phraotes of India to value friends above gold or silver, and Pound rhymes that conversation with Mencius's advice to King Hwuy Leang ("Huey" in Pound's slangy updating): true value is gained, as the ideograms indicate, "by wealth put to use, not by treasure accumulated."

Following Apollonius' travels through India, the Near East, and then back to the Mediterranean, Pound lingers on an episode that reflects upon the scene in Canto 1—Apollonius' conversation with the ghost of Achilles on a mound in Troy:

> That he passed the night on the mound of Achilles
> "master of tempest and fire"
>   & he set up Palamedes
> an image that I, Philostratus, saw
>   and a shrine that will hold ten people drinking.
> "It was not by ditch-digging and sheep's-guts . . .
>   "in Aeolis close to Methymna"
> in the summer lightning, close upon cock-crow.   (94/638)

As Wilhelm observes, this not only recalls Odysseus' dialogue with Tiresias but reminds us that the whole of The Cantos is "an extended dialogue with the dead."[6] During his interview with Achilles, Apollonius can ask five questions, one of which is why Homer never mentions Palamedes, the inventor of the alphabet and a hero to "all preservers of tradition" like Apollonius and Pound. Achilles explains that because Palamedes saw through the madness that Odysseus feigned to dodge the Trojan War, Odysseus later killed him out of jealousy, and Homer, to keep his hero unblemished, ignores Palamedes altogether. Even Homer, therefore, is implicated in the historical black-out, and Achilles asks Apollonius to build a shrine for Palamedes, much as Elpenor beseeched Odysseus to set up a monumental oar. Philostratus then breaks into his narrative with an eyewitness testimonial: he has seen the shrine that Apollonius built and it is big enough to hold ten people. Philostratus' *Life* is a metaphor for that shrine, a textual monument he has erected to Apollonius to preserve the sage from the historical black-out, and Pound restores that monument by recasting Conybeare's translation. These textual transmissions, like the *nekuia*, open up channels with the dead, though Apollonius boasts that his canalizing did not require the clumsy "ditch-digging" of Odysseus.

We do get some literal ditch-digging, however, when Apollonius travels to Greece to see a fellow philosopher, "Musonius, / the man with the spade" (94/639). Musonius had been arrested by Nero and sent to join a slave labor gang that was digging the Corinth Canal between the Aegean and Adriatic seas; defiantly, he tells Apollonius he prefers such Greek canalizing to Nero's Rome. The image of Musonius' "spade" mirrors the inverted spade at the end of Canto 88, linking him with all the other diggers into the past who are symbolized by Epstein's "Rock-Drill" sculpture. Just as he built a shrine to Palamedes, Apollonius raises a "stele" to Musonius, another metaphor for the many textual monuments to archivists and editors who fought the historical black-out. Apollonius himself felt that black-out "in the time of Domitian" (91/616), when he was put on trial and told he would have to plead his case in court without any documents. Pound, who was similarly stripped of texts when he was imprisoned in Pisa, relishes Apollonius' wry query as to whether he was entering a courthouse or a "bath-house"; stressing the sexual innuendoes in the scene, Pound praises Apollonius as a "young man" who "declined to be buggar'd" (91/616). Apollonius got revenge for himself and for Musonius when he traveled to Egypt and persuaded Vespasian to overthrow Nero and establish a succession of good emperors, the Roman equivalent of a vital Confucian dynasty:

> VESPASIAN a.D. 69
>
> . . . .
>
> ANTONINUS reigned 138 to 161
> SEVERUS and Julia Domna about 198   (94/639-40)

It was this Julia who commissioned Philostratus to write the *Life of Apollonius*, rescuing the sage from the historical black-out imposed by the Church's henchmen, like that "schnorrer Euphrates" who had written a tract against Apollonius.

In Canto 96, the first Canto of *Thrones*, Pound continues his documentary odyssey of the Mediterranean world by shifting to another collection he calls "Migne 95" (96/652).[7] If Ezra Pound had a double in the nineteenth century, it would have to be Jacques Paul Migne. A priest forced out of his native Orleans because he had written a controversial book about the priesthood,

Migne went to Paris where, after failing at journalism, he acquired a printing-house and began churning out cheap editions of the Church fathers' works—much as Pound was issuing his Square Dollar reprints of economic documents from St. Elizabeths. Migne managed to publish 224 volumes of his *Patrologiae Cursus Completus* before he was blacked-out by a fire, by Church censorship, and by shortages caused by the Franco-Prussian War. His documents still fill hefty stretches of library shelving and remain a valuable scholarly tool despite their rough editing and uneven translations. The 95th volume, which Pound acquired after completing his own 95th Canto, contains Bede's chronicle and two historical collections, *The History of the Langobards* and *The Mixed History*, compiled by another fascinating archivist, Paul the Deacon.

Like Migne and Pound, Paul worked largely from secondhand documents to produce *The History of the Langobards*, which has been described as a "vessel of tradition in a period of chaos." An eighth-century Benedictine monk from Lombardy, he was one of the last western Europeans to speak Greek; in addition, he served as court scholar for Charlemagne, who assigned to him the Migne-like task of collecting the homilies of the Church fathers. In his old age Paul returned to his native land—much as Pound, after his release from St. Elizabeths, went to live in northern Italy with his daughter and her husband, a descendant of the Lombards. The *History of the Langobards*, which Paul completed in these last years, was an important historical manuscript and printed book from the Middle Ages to the seventeenth century, but it fell into obscurity in modern times. Because it marked the transmission of classical culture into northern Italy, however, Pound wanted to resurrect the document and return it to wider circulation.

He begins with a quote from one of Paul's poems,

Tellus vomit cadavera (96/651)

These corpses vomited up by the earth take us back to the nekuia of Canto 1, where Odysseus summoned the "Souls out of Erebus" (1/3). Like Andreas Divus, Paul the Deacon is himself one of those spirits, now conjured by Pound, who reaches back for Paul's voice as it recounts the migrations of the Lombard people from Scandinavia, through Yugoslavia, and into northern Italy. The tale of the first Lombard king, who slew his enemy, married his daughter, and then invited "his wife to drink from her father's skull" (96/651), recalls classical myths and troubadour legends from earlier Cantos. When Paul interrupts his narrative to describe the "cup which I, Paulus, saw" (96/651), Pound splices the *History* with the *Life of Apollonius*, where Philostratus affirmed that he had seen the shrine his master had built for Palamedes. These eyewitness notes resurrect the voices of the editors, and soon we hear Paul tracing his own family's roots in Poundian slang:

> and my grand-dad got out of what is now Jugoslavia
> with a bow, arrows and a wolf acting as guide
> till it thought gramp looked too hungry   (96/652)

That oral flavor spills over into Paul's celebration of King Rothar, who "got some laws written down" (96/652)—the first great document of Lombard culture. "A prolog" to this law code contained a history of the Lombards, a self-reflexive image of Paul's own history like those Pound focuses on in other documents.

After tracing a line of Lombard kings whose love for gold literally as well as figuratively dragged them down—"auro gravatus" (96/652)—Paul focuses on the great king Luitprand, who brought Lombard culture to its height in the eighth century. The document Paul selects to mark this point in his *History* is the "ACTUM TICINI IN PALATIO" (96/653), the record of an "act performed in the palace" in 744, whereby Luitprand resigned and officially transmitted his power to his successor, Hildeprand. Pound connects that documentary register of the orderly transmission of power with "a stone in Modena by the ambon" (96/653), which records the coronation rites for Lombard kings. At this point the Migne editor of Paul's *History of the Langobards* breaks into his text to affirm, like Philostratus and Paul, that he himself has seen this stone. As a primitive register of the orderly transmission of power, this stone provides Pound with a metaphor for the transmission of cultural documents.

Pound now shifts to another of Paul's texts in "Migne 95," the *Historia Miscella*, or *Mixed History*. This was originally a ten-volume chronicle of Roman history written by the fourth-century Latin historian Eutropius. Paul had given the work as a present to one of his pupils, the daughter of the Lombard king Desiderius. When the princess complained—rather remarkably—that Eutropius' *History* was too short, Paul expanded the work with six additional volumes that brought the chronicle up to the fall of the Goths in Italy. He had intended to continue on to the rise of the Lombards, but his work was interrupted by history itself—the rise of the Carolingian empire in the west, which conquered Lombardy, confiscated Paul's family's property, and imprisoned his brother. Paul himself served at Charlemagne's court, and only after returning to his native Lombardy did he take up the *Mixed History* again, intertwining the chronicle with accounts of the Lombards, the Franks, and the Eastern Empire.

Like Kung, who said "I transmit, I do not create," Paul was a "compiler" who tried "to collect and transmit in more convenient form what was at hand, not to create anything new."[8] Moving as erratically as Pound did through a variety of older documents, Paul threw historical sequence "into confusion" by cutting back and forth among sources and juxtaposing fragments "very loosely without natural connection." Another self-reflexive image for *The Cantos*, the *Mixed History* was a "rag-bag" of documents that stood for 1,000 years as an important chronicle, but then passed out of favor because it was too derivative, often reproducing older texts word-for-word. Still, Pound (whose epic is open to the same criticism) saw the *History* as a vital link between western Europe and the ancient world and Paul as a canalizer whose knowledge of classical literature did "not occur again in the same breadth and fulness before the time of the Renaissance."[9] Paul's continuation of Eutropius' *History* was, in turn, extended around 1000 A.D. by Landulph, who added a history of the Eastern Roman Empire.

Through this multilayered text, Pound works his way back to the *Life of Apollonius*. Beginning with the section of the *Mixed History* compiled by Eutropius, he marks the reign of "DIOCLETIAN, 37th after Augustus" (96/653) according to Eutropius' system of counting, then moves on to the reigns of "Vespasiano," "Antoninus," and Septimius Severus, reminding us that it was "Severus' wife" who "spoke to Philostratus about the biography" of Apollonius (96/654). The revitalized Rome shaped by these emperors was inspired by Apollonius and, as Pound interprets the *Mixed History*, maintained by governmental control of the economy. Having traced the migration of that dynastic spirit westward, through Paul's Lombards, Pound now moves eastward to Constantinople, where the classical culture reflowered after Rome fell to "Pictorum, / Vandali" (96/654). Working from Landulph's segment of the *Mixed History*, Pound celebrates the documentary symbol of Byzantine culture, the law code of the emperor Justinian:

> Mirabile brevitate correxit, says Landulph
> of Justinian's Code   (97/682)

Justinian's careful construction of that document mirrors his building of "Sta Sophia," and both monuments mark the triumph of Constantinople over the "money sellers" who "thought they would bump off Justinian" (96/654). Justinian's daughter-in-law "Sophia Augusta," who "made the money-sellers cough up something or other" (96/655), maintained the economic control vital to Byzantine culture, as did another dynasty of good emperors—Justinian II, "MAURICIUS" (96/655), and "HERACLIUS" (96/656).

Pound caps his adaptation of the *Mixed History* with another document, reproduced exactly as he found it on column 1060 of Migne's 95th volume:

> Anno sexto imperii sui Justinianus (the second)
> pacem, quam ad Habdimelich habuit, ex amentia
> dissolvit, et omnem Cypriorum insulam, et populum
> irrationabiliter voluit transmigrare, et characterem

> qui missus fuerat ab Habdimelich, eum noviter visus
> esset . . . et his auditis Habdimelich satanice
> stimulatus rogabat ne pax solveretur, sed susciperent
> monetam suam, cum Arabes non susciperent Romanorum
> incisionem in suis nummis. Verum dato pondere
> auri ait: Nullum Romanis damnum efficitur, ex eo
> quod Arabes nova cuderent . . .
> Quod et factum est, et misit Habdimelich ad aedifi-
> candum templum Muchan, et voluit auferre columnas . . .
>   —col. 1060, The Deacon, Migne's Patroligia.   (96/658)

In this edict Emperor Justinian II insists that the Arab leader Habdimelich pay tribute in Byzantine coins, and Pound regards the document as evidence for the claim of an American economic historian, Alexander Del Mar, that the success of the Byzantine empire was based on control of credit and coinage. "This item," Pound says, endured through the centuries and, as he believed could happen with all vital documents, was put into action to transform society when Mustafa "Kemal" used it "in our time" (96/658) for his new Turkey.

The preservation and transmission of such vital documents, once again, is as much Pound's subject as the history recorded in those documents, and these Cantos, like the shrine that Apollonius erected to Palamedes, constitute his "memorial to archivists and librarians" (96/654) such as Philostratus, Paul the Deacon, and Jacques Paul Migne. One of the most intriguing documents unearthed "down somewhere under all of this" is "the Eparch's book" (96/654) of the great Byzantine emperor Leo VI (866-912).[10] Pound thought "That bit from the Eparch's edict," along with the coinage edict of Justinian II, were the documentary pillars of Byzantine culture, and he devoted the rest of Canto 96 to a redaction of Leo's text. Nicknamed "The Wise" because of his scholarly background, Leo was a great creator and transmitter of documents, as was his father, Basil, who "had revived work on the great *Corpus Juris* of Justinian and created the voluminous code known as the Basilica." Leo completed his father's code and enforced it as "the law of the land," adding on his own "113 separate edicts on matters of civil and church discipline."[11]

The *Edict of the Eparch* was designed for the emperor's special administrator—who was akin to a mayor—for Constantinople. Its twenty-two sections lay down regulations for all of the important trades and businesses: notaries, gold- and silversmiths, bankers, silk merchants, perfumers, chandlers, grocers, saddlers, butchers, and so on. These detailed regulations constitute an "eloquent testimonial to the internal order of Byzantium, with the State having absolute power over all industrial and commercial activities."[12] The unfolding regulations, trade by trade, form a textual analogue for those Venetian parades of guildsmen Pound celebrated in Canto 26 as symbols of the well-run community. While Pound is obviously fascinated with the image of a fully-regulated state, especially one where bankers and gold-dealers are kept in check, he is also intrigued with the Eparch's edict as a text. Like so many of the documents in *The Cantos*, the original edict was lost and only a fourteenth-century manuscript copy—which is particularly hard to decipher—survives. It was found in Greece in 1636 by a Dutch embassy chaplain, who gave it to a wealthy Swiss lawyer, who, in turn, willed the *Edict* to the Geneva University Library, where it lay unexamined for three centuries.

In the 1890s, however, this "precious document" was resurrected by Professor Jules Nicole, whose translation and publication of it was a major factor in the revival of Byzantine studies and in the recognition of Constantinople as a vital center for the preservation of classical culture throughout the Middle Ages.[13] The text itself, as Nicole published it, was just the sort of crazy-quilt that Pound loved—a segment of the Greek set against a modern Greek translation with Latin and French translations side by side, and, underneath, numerous footnotes registering "Professor Nicole's annoyance" (96/664) with the puzzling technical and archaic vocabulary. Pound, as usual, zigzags through all these linguistic layers, quibbling with Professor Nicole, offering his own suggestions for translations, and even tossing in Chinese ideograms to help nail down the meaning of a word like *Megalozelon*. The word, as Pound notes at the beginning of his adaptation of the *Edict*, is not found in "Dr. Liddell's" (96/658) Greek dictionary. It puzzled Professor Nicole, who translated it into the Latin "Hyacinthinis" (96/658), trying to capture the shade of meaning in a word that specifies the distinctive shades of red and purple silk that merchants were to reserve for royalty. "Why not fake purple," Pound suggests, reaching into colloquial speech for a sharper translation, then cutting to the ideograms "tzu" (purple), "chih" (goes far to), "to" (surpass), "chu" (red) (96/659)—not so strange a shift when we recall that Byzantine silk workers were adapting this Chinese industry.

Pound's rock-drilling through the layers of Nicole's translation demonstrates, as Wilhelm has observed, "the difficulty of getting at an original text through a translator and one or two intermediate languages."[14] Once again Pound joins the company of editors and scholars such as "Ducange" (96/659), Norman Holmes "Pearson" (96/662), and "Morrison, / de Saumase, de Reitz" (96/662) dedicated to the "refinement of language" (96/659). Such verbal alchemists, like the Byzantine goldsmiths regulated by the *Edict*, construct an edifice out of language that endures like the city itself. These artificers are reflected in the *Edict*'s regulations for the notaries of Constantinople, and Pound recasts the order of the document to highlight the role of these verbal contractors in the life of the city. In the *Edict*, the notaries are described in the first set of regulations, but Pound skips right to the fourth section, concerning the silk merchants, and continues through regulations against "hoarding" for grocers, buying "sheep" for "Xoirempers" (pork butchers), price fixing for "bakers," closing times for "TAVERNERS" (96/660), on through to the 22nd section, which regulates "contractors for fine work, plaster, / marble, askothurariōn, paint & the rest of 'em" (96/662).

A pun on "contractors" leads back to the opening section with its proscriptions for the "notary," who "must have some general culture or he will / make a mess of the contracts" (96/664-65):

> To be tabulary, must know the Manuale
> to recite it, and the Basiliks, 60 books
> and draw up an act in the presence, and be sponsored
> by the primicier and his colleagues
> and have a clear Handschrift
> and be neither babbler nor insolent, nor sloppy in habits
> and have a style. Without perfect style
> might not notice punctuation and phrases
> that alter the sense,
> and if he writes down a variant
> his sponsors will be responsible.
> Give him time to show what he's got.   (96/666)

Like Tiresias, the notary of Byzantium must hold the documents of his culture in memory and be able to recite them, as well as write in a manner that will manifest his character. Upon the clarity and purity of the notary's language, which serves as a model for all other trades, the edifice of Byzantine culture depends.

In Cantos 98 and 99 Pound rhymes the *Edict of the Eparch* with the *Sacred Edict* issued by the Chinese emperor K'ang Hsi in 1670.[15] Like the Byzantine emperor, K'ang intended his document as a practical guide for individual and governmental conduct, and it was hung in all the law courts of the land. As another many-layered palimpsest, the *Sacred Edict* interests Pound as much by its texture as its substance. K'ang's original edict consisted of sixteen, tersely stated Confucian maxims, but his son, "Iong Ching" (Yung Chêng), thought the maxims needed clarification, so in 1724 he expanded them into a book with a chapter on each maxim, all in the elegant literary style of "Uen-li" (98/690). Pound sees this textual transformation as a reflection of the filial piety at the core of the best Chinese dynasties, and the fact that K'ang and Yung are the last two emperors treated in the *Comprehensive Mirror* ties these late Cantos to the Dynastic Cantos (53-61).

The next metamorphosis of the *Sacred Edict* came at the hands of another Poundian "double"—"Ouang, the Commissioner" of the Salt Works in "Shensi" province (98/686). Ouang, or "Wang" as Pound chummily calls him, was bothered that the *Sacred Edict*, whether in K'ang's terse maxims or Yung's elegant expansion, was not reaching the masses. With typically Poundian brass, Wang rewrote the *Edict* "in volgar' eloquio taking the sense down to the people" (98/688), just as Dante had done when he switched from Latin to the language of his native Tuscany. Savoring the commissioner's plain speech, Pound recasts it into salty English:

> And if your kids don't study, that's your fault.
> Tell 'em. Don't kid yourself, and don't lie.   (99/705)

At times it seems to be Wang who is speaking through Ezra Pound: "Teach 'em classics not hog-wash" (99/704).[16]

The next link in this chain of documentary transmission and transformation is Frederick Baller, a missionary to China who published a translation of the *Sacred Edict* in 1892—about the same time Professor Jules Nicole was preparing his edition of the *Edict of the Eparch*. Baller found the Sacred Edict a "thesaurus of everyday words, phrases and idioms" that was rare in Chinese literature, most of which was written in "Uen-li."[17] Thus it was ideal for the practical task of training missionaries to China in "understanding the common people."[18] Yet Baller's own English translation is done in genteel English, and Pound, like Wang, must make new the *Sacred Edict* for his own age:

> and our debt here is to Baller
> and to *volgar' eloquio.*
>   Despite Mathews this Wang was a stylist.
> Uen-li will not help you talk to them,
>   Iong-ching republished the edict
> But the salt-commisioner took it down to the people
>   who, in Baller's view, speak in quotations;
>   think in quotations   (98/690)

Always the rock-driller, Pound wants to recover the voices of the dead beneath the written text, so he probes for a spoken vocabulary that can no more be found in Mathews' standard Chinese dictionary than the words of Leo the Wise could in the Greek dictionary of "Dr. Liddell" (96/658). The line of textual transmission that stretches from K'ang through Pound is reflected in Chinese culture itself, which preserves the past in oral documents—thinking and speaking in quotations, so that the Chinese people themselves constitute a living archive.

To pump blood back into those voices, Pound circulates among the layers of his text, "tracing the progress of this tradition in the three different styles of the *Edict.*"[19] First he gives the original maxims of K'ang, each of which consisted of just seven characters, trying to recapture the compressed "meaning of the Emperor" by such stark translations as "heart's-tone-think-say" (98/691) and pithy equivalents like

II. Ten thousand years say men have clans and descendents.
III. There are districts. Avoid litigation.
IV. Without grain you will not eat or tend silkworms,
     Imperial paradigm was by ploughing.   (98/691-92)

Into some maxims Pound weaves the homespun tone of Poor Richard—"V.
and then waste not, / Nor scrape iron off the point of a needle"
(98/692)—whose voice exemplifies the very economy it recommends by not
wasting words.

In Canto 99 Pound shifts to the voice of K'ang's son, Yung Chêng, that
"literary kuss" (61/340), as he is called in the Dynastic Cantos. From Yung's
preface to his version of the *Sacred Edict*, Pound tries to recapture the
metaphoric play with which the son amplified his father's maxims. Yung
describes his edition as a "promulgating" (*chiang*) and "amplifying" (*kuang*) of
the *Sacred Edict*. As David Gordon explains, in the *chiang* ideogram Pound
discerned "an element" that looked like "intertwining trellis work" and
resembled "the 'blue grass' radical"; similarly, he saw that the ideogram *kuang*
"has within it the 'yellow' radical" *hsien* reproduced at the conclusion of Canto
98.[20] *Hsien*, in turn, is composed of the radicals for "sun" and "silk cord";
therefore, Pound can begin with the "silk cords of the sunlight," punningly
transform it into "Chords of the sunlight" (98/693), and then reweave its
imagistic roots:

> Till the blue grass turn yellow
>   and the yellow leaves float in air
> And Iong Cheng (Canto 61)
>   of the line of Kang Hi
> by the silk cords of the sunlight   (99/694)

In recasting Yung's renewal of his father's text, Pound fastens on the "sun"
radical that, in the Dynastic Cantos, figured in the maxim, "MAKE IT NEW"
(53/265); here, just as the *sun* renews itself each day, so the *son* Yung reweaves
his father's text in an act of filial piety that continues through the fabric of
Pound's poem.

As Canto 99 develops, the crusty voice of Wang keeps breaking through
Yung's elegance until it finally emerges in all its "vulgar" eloquence:

> Fools fall for weapons and poison,
>   You are not all of you idiots,
>   There are a lot of you who will not
>   fall for this hokum.
> But your females like to burn incense
> and buzz round in crowds and processions   (99/701)

Like Odysseus, Pound has had to dig down for Wang's voice beneath the genteel surface of Baller's translation—transfusing Baller's pallid "Instruct the Rising Generation, with a view to prevent Evil Doing" with new blood to get Wang's "XI Teach kids to keep out of mischief" (99/704):[21]

> Dress 'em in folderols
> > and feed 'em with dainties
> In the end they will sell out the homestead.   (99/705)

What you teach 'em, as Pound has said from the beginning, is "classics" (99/704) like the *Sacred Edict* itself, whose texture reflects the virtues of clarity, economy, and order that can keep a society new. Those classics, however, must themselves be perpetually made new by new generations of archivists, editors, and scholars like those Pound commemorates throughout these final Cantos.

Final Documents: Coke and Rock

It was not until 1957, after nearly a decade in St. Elizabeths, that Pound discovered Sir Edward Coke's *Second Institutes*, or, as he abbreviates it in Coke's own legal style, "Coke. Inst. 2" (107/756).[1] The collection of forty documents, many of which treat freedom from unjust imprisonment, traced the metamorphoses of *Magna Charta*. The fact that Coke's *Institutes* were not more widely known was, for Pound, yet another instance of the historical black-out. Once again he went to work, not only condensing the *Institutes* into Cantos 107, 108, and 109 but issuing Coke's commentary on *Magna Charta* in a separate volume in his Square Dollar series of cheap reprints.

"The history of *Magna Charta*," like that of most documents in *The Cantos*, is one of "repeated re-interpretation."[2] The original charter, granted by King John at Runnymede, was essentially a feudal document with specific provisions for barons, the agricultural and commercial classes, and the Church. Its importance lay not so much in these provisions but in its very nature as a document—a text that superseded even the power of the king—and in its organic power to grow, renew itself, and spawn other vital texts. Sir Edward Coke, its greatest transmitter and transformer, did not even know *Magna Charta* in its original version but worked from its reissue in 1225 by King John's successor, Henry III; this is the same secondhand document that Pound had dreamed of in the prison camp at Pisa:

> To watch a while from the tower
> > where dead flies lie thick over the old charter
> forgotten, oh quite forgotten
> but confirming John's first one,
> and still there if you climb over attic rafters   (80/514)

Imprisoned himself, both at Pisa and St. Elizabeths, Pound tried to free that ancient document by retracing Coke's account of its metamorphoses through a long line of English kings and parliaments. Like the *Sacred Edict*, *Magna Charta* became a "sacred text, glossed, interpreted and extended" by scholars like Coke who "took it down to the people" in their day as Pound now hoped to do in his.[3]

Characteristically, Pound makes *Magna Charta* as much the hero of these Cantos as Coke himself. Its organic power of "unfolding more meaning as it confronts new circumstances" makes the document seem like a huge "azalea" that has "grown while we sleep" (107/756) or a "great algae" (107/762) that underlies all living forms. He compares the document to the multitextured tapestries of "dutch weavers in Norwich" (107/761), where Coke spent his childhood. Because the latent power of this document (like the resources Adams found in the colonial charter of Massachusetts) "only awaits an intelligent interpretation," Coke was able to trace a "continuous thread in English law" that was rooted in pre-Norman customs. While Coke's belief that law "had grown up with the Trees, Herbs, and Grass" is criticized by modern legal historians, Pound saw it as a Confucian awareness of the organic nature of civic order. In the leaves of the *Institutes*, where many "ancient and other statutes" were brought together in parallel columns of Latin and English along with Coke's own intricate commentaries, Pound also saw a mirror of the multitextured documents in the Chinese Cantos.[4]

He begins with Coke's "Proeme" praising King Henry III, who, in the twentieth year of his reign, reaffirmed both *Magna Charta* and the *"Charta de Foresta,"* thus resisting the advice of "evil counsellors" who had urged him to cancel both of these vital documents:

> Coke. Inst. 2..
>   to all cathedral churches to be
>   read 4 times in the yeare
> 20. H. 3
>   that is certainty   (107/756)

Here a vital document is taken down to the people, read aloud at seasonal rituals; Coke's translation and commentary, like Wang's version of the *Sacred Edict*, recaptures that colloquial power. Because they possessed *Magna Charta*, the English people could resist the Stuarts, "that slobbering bugger Jim First" and his son "Charlie" (107/757), while the French, without such a document, could not pull off a successful revolution:

> Voltaire could not do it;
> the french could not do it.
>   they had not Magna Charta   (107/757-58)

"That charter" is "the root" (107/757) of English liberty, and Pound underscores the organic image with the Chinese ideogram *pen* (root), a juxtaposition of English phrase and Chinese ideogram that sets up a series of verbal and visual puns cutting across Latin, Chinese, and American slang. The *pen* is both etymological "root" and organic source of texts, mightier than any sword, "our PIVOT" (107/759), Pound says, equivalent to the Confucian classic *Chung Yung* (*The Unwobbling Pivot*), which balances the power of the king with the rights of the people. In the Latin formula the king used when he signed these charters, Pound sees an image of the vital grip the people had on the king through these charters:

> his testibus . . .
>   were call'd chartae.
> That is our PIVOT   (107/759)

The charters that hold the king's "testibus" echo the phallic shape of the *pen* ideogram and recall Pound's praise of "Wang," the Salt Commissioner whose "phallic heart" (99/697) went into the *Sacred Edict*.

The documents that flowered from *Magna Charta*—regulations on fishing and farming, importing and exporting, taxes and duties, dowries and wardships—make Coke's *Second Institutes*, like the *Edict of the Eparch*, a blueprint that regulates every aspect of communal life. Quoting from the *Statutum de Marlebridge*, enacted in "One thousand two sixty seven," Pound notes that it renewed the rights of *Magna Charta* to all people, "as well high as low" (107/760); then he links Coke's comment on the statute, "Sapiens incipit a fine" (a wise man begins with his end in mind), with the ideograms for "ends" and "beginnings" (107/760). The Confucian prescription for complete order prompts Pound to consider Coke's own beginnings and ends, from his early years in Norwich to his career in London.

As a young lawyer in 1612, Coke attacked a writ, "de heretico comburendo" (107/761), which allowed a bishop's court to execute heretics. Against Sir Francis Bacon, he argued that the writ violated *Magna Charta*'s guarantee that a person could refuse to testify about his religious beliefs. In 1621 Coke was himself imprisoned for defending freedom of speech against King James, who had tried to punish Londoners for calling the Spanish ambassador "Gondemar" a "Devil in dung-cart" (107/762). In 1628, in the midst of a scandal in which his own daughter was convicted of adultery and sentenced to walk "In a white sheet in the Savoy" (107/761), Coke fought King Charles' effort to levy a tax without parliamentary consent. When the king threatened to imprison anyone who did not pay, Coke fought the writ of "*habeas*" (107/761) with the statute "25 Edward III" (108/764), which forbade unjust imprisonment. The king eventually relented and issued the "Petition of Right" that reaffirmed individual liberties:

> From the Charter to the Petition
>   in June and toward twilight
>   DROIT FAIT   (108/764)

The king's official "DROIT FAIT," accepting the petition, was greeted by a great communal celebration, like those that attended the Monte charters and the Leopoldine decrees.

The "Petition of Right" reconfirmed an earlier document, the "*Statutum Tallagio*" (107/764), which guaranteed freedom from unjust taxation and was included in Coke's *Second Institutes*. The "*Statutum Tallagio*" had been renewed once before, by Edward I's "Confirmationis / Chartorum" (108/766) issued in 1297 after Edward had had to abandon his efforts to tax the barons and agree that taxes could only be levied under a parliamentary grant. The Confirmation Charter also made *Magna Charta* and other documents the "guier" (guide) to justice throughout England, and it was read aloud to the people "twice a year" (108/766). Pound celebrates the power of this text to limit the king by reproducing its closing phrases:

> nous lettres ouverts
>   nostre fits a Londres le x jour Doctobre
>   the five and 20th year   (108/766)

The same principle of no taxation ("nullum tallagium") without the consent of free men ("liberorum") was renewed by the next document in Coke's *Institutes*, "De Tallagio non cencendo," which was wrung from Edward in the "34th year" of his reign (108/766) just as later it would inspire the colonists of Massachusetts in their battle against George III.

Proceeding through the documents in the *Institutes*, Pound finds the "articuli super Chartas," which, like Henry III's renewal of *Magna Charta*, was read "4 times the year" on "Michael, Xmas, Easter, Saint John" (108/767). The seasonal festivals when the charters are taken down to the people are like ancient rites that bind the community to the rhythms of nature. "Articuli" extended the freedoms of earlier charters and guaranteed that constitutional violations "be tried locally." Thus, when Charles I "kept this seven years under the hatches / 1634-'41" (108/767), his oppression violated both constitutional and natural orders, just as Coke's struggle to free the ancient documents became a mythic battle to restore communal vitality. In 1641, the year that Charles' illegal tax was abolished, Coke's *Commentary* on *Magna Charta* was approved for publication.

>   Elfynge
>   Cler
>   Domus
>   Com
>   (108/768)

Pound here reproduces the inscription of the clerk of the House of Commons clearing Coke's *Commentary* for publication—a victory over the historical black-out that spurred a great revolution and confirmed Pound's belief that cultural regeneration can follow the renewal and dissemination of vital texts.

Pound's choice for the last document in his palimpsest, Joseph Rock's *Ancient Na-Khi Kingdom of Southwest China*, returns him to the primitive world that opened Canto I.[5] Rock, an American botanist and anthropologist, in the 1920s began a lifelong study of the Na-Khi (black man) tribe in the mountains of southwest China. His research, like that of all the heroes of *The Cantos* from Kung to Coke, was a collecting, editing, and making new of earlier documents—the rites, myths, and stone inscriptions that constitute the archive of this ancient culture. Rock relied upon a Tiresias-like tribal priest who had preserved the oral documents of his tribe and could decipher its pictographic relics. From these sources he compiled eighteen volumes of notebooks about the Na-Khi and intended to transmit these cultural records to the rest of the world, but, after twenty years of labor, his research suffered the black-out that had expunged so many ancient records and, Pound feared, would someday blot out *The Cantos*: like "Novvy's ship" (23/107) that went down with its cargo of precious Greek manuscripts, the ship carrying Rock's notebooks to America was sunk by the Japanese in 1944:

> Bunting and Upward neglected,
>   all the resisters blacked out,
> From time's wreckage shored,
>   these fragments shored against ruin,

and the sun 日 jih[4-5]
>   new with the day.
> Mr Rock still hopes to climb at Mount Kinabalu
> his fragments sunk (20 years)   (110/781)

Like the sun that renews itself each day, Rock heroically began his research again and produced *The Ancient Na-Khi Kingdom* of *Southwest China*, along with monographs on Na-Khi rituals.

In his final Cantos, Pound renews both Rock and his own poem by drawing upon images and events in *The Ancient Na-Khi Kingdom* that recall figures from earlier Cantos. He notes, for example, that "Kublai, / Te Te of Ch'eng, called Timur" (101/723) conquered the Na-Khi tribe in 1247—at about the same time that Marco Polo forged Europe's link with China. Among the photographs in Rock's book is one of a Na-Khi maiden who seems to be another incarnation of that goddess whose metamorphic beauty has been transformed

through *The Cantos* from the moment Aphrodite emerged from the Latin of
Andreas Divus:

> With the sun and moon on her shoulders,
>   the star-discs sewn on her coat
>   at Li Chiang, the snow range   (101/726)

So, too, Rock's journey through the Na-Khi countryside becomes another of
the many *periploi* in *The Cantos*, the Chinese rivers and mountains recalling
such sites as the river "Achiloös" and "Mont Ségur" (101/725).

> And over Li Chiang, the snow range is turquoise
> Rock's world that he saved us for memory
>   a thin trace in high air   (112/786)

Li Chiang, which Rock considered "one of the most interesting" districts and
"certainly the most beautiful" in the Na-Khi province, becomes for Pound
another kingdom of the mind, like the city of Dioce, its trace carved in human
memory.[6]

Rock's precise and delicate translations of the ancient records he gleaned
from the old scholars of Li Chiang also transmit the whispering language of the
Na-Khi, a "talk made out of wind noise" (104/738), which the Na-Khi
huntsmen developed so that their speech would not disturb the game.[7] Such
an organic language, born from the community's relation to nature, echoes
Yeats's "I made it out of a mouthful of air" and places Rock's work in that
tradition of documents that preserve and renew the dead voices of the past.
That tradition finds its emblem in Rock's description of a temple dedicated to
Lung Wang, the Dragon King:

> By the pomegranate water,
>   in the clear air
>   over Li Chiang
> The firm voice amid pine wood,
>   many springs are at the foot of
>   Hsiang Shan
> By the temple pool, Lung Wang's
>   the clear discourse
>   as Jade stream   (112/784)

Even as Pound celebrates the clarity of ancient discourse, his own voice
invokes the triadic line of William Carlos Williams's late poetry. The temple's
jade stream symbolizes an endless flow of speech transmitted from past to

present, a stream that opened, in *The Cantos*, when Odysseus dug a bloody fosse to give voice to Tiresias.

Pound traces that stream in the course of the Yangtze River, which makes a great loop in the Li Chiang district "by the waters of Stone Drum" (101/726), a Na-Khi village named after a primitive stone drum upon which a sixteenth-century conqueror inscribed a hymn of his victories. Rock took rubbings of these stone pictographs and offered his own translation of the hymn. The first pictograph, according to his translation, describes how the troops marched "with the air of a tiger or a plumed bird," and Pound recasts Rock's translation by isolating the two images:

> the first moon is the tiger's,
>   Pheasant calls out of bracken   (101/726)

Such an imagist nuance is Pound's figurative rubbing of Rock, as Rock had taken his impression of the Stone Drum. This process of preserving and renewing documents involves yet another rock—a stone, supposedly inscribed by "Kublai" (101/723), outside of a pagoda he had erected in a remote Na-Khi village. When Rock examined this stone, however, he found that time had worn off the inscription, but the text had been recopied on the walls of the pagoda itself.

That act of recopying an ancient document anticipates Rock's own dedicated preservation of Na-Khi records; it also looks forward to the question Pound asks at the end of *The Cantos*: "who will copy this palimpsest?" (116/797). His nearly paranoiac fears of the historical black-out reflect his concern that his own poetry endure, a concern that drove him to devote his *Cantos* to copying the texts of other scribes, a concern that here, at the end of the poem, reminds him of his dependence upon the Cokes and Rocks and Kungs of the future:

> But the record
>   the palimpsest—
> a little light
>   in great darkness—   (116/795)

His own vast document of documents becomes a "great ball of crystal," which Pound at the end of *The Cantos* passes on to another generation of archivists. Such a "great acorn of light" (116/795) in the hands of canalizers who "make it flow thru," can lead a culture, he believed, "like a rushlight," "back to splendour" (116/797).

Notes and References

PREFACE

1. Ezra Pound, "I gather the Limbs of Osiris," *Selected Prose 1909-1965*, ed. William Cookson (New York: New Directions, 1973), p. 22.

CHAPTER I: LINES OF TRANSMISSION

1. All references to *The Cantos* are noted parenthetically in the text by canto number/page number in *The Cantos of Ezra Pound* (New York: New Directions, 1973).

2. Pound, "The Jefferson-Adams Letters as a Shrine and a Monument," in *Impact: Essays on Ignorance and the Decline of American Civilization*, ed. Noel Stock (Chicago: Henry Regnery, 1960), p. 166.

3. Eva Hesse, "Books Behind *The Cantos*, Part One," *Paideuma* 1 (1972): 145.

4. Quoted in Noel Stock, *The Life of Ezra Pound* (New York: Pantheon, 1970), pp. 457-58.

5. I am greatly indebted to many of these articles, and I acknowledge that indebtedness with a general footnote at the beginning of my interpretation of Pound's use of each historical document.

6. J. Hillis Miller, Introduction, *Bleak House*, by Charles Dickens (London: Penguin, 1971), p. 11.

7. *Literary Essays of Ezra Pound* (Norfolk: New Directions, 1934), p. 86.

8. For deconstructionist readings of *The Cantos* see Joseph Riddel, "Pound and the Decentered Image," *Georgia Review* 29 (1975): 565-91, and Marjorie Perloff, *The Poetics of Indeterminacy* (Princeton: Princeton University Press, 1981), pp. 180-99.

9. *Literary Essays of Ezra Pound*, p. 259.

10. *Guide to Kulchur* (Norfolk: New Directions, 1938), p. 24.

11. George Dekker, *Sailing After Knowledge: "The Cantos of Ezra Pound," A Critical Appraisal* (London: Routledge, 1963), p. 16.

12. *The Spirit of Romance* (New York: New Directions, 1968), p. 15.

13. Ronald Bush, *The Genesis of Ezra Pound's Cantos* (Princeton: Princeton University Press, 1976), p. 129.

14. *Letters of Ezra Pound 1907-1941*, ed. D.D. Paige (New York: Harcourt, Brace and World, 1950), p. 274.

15. Hugh Kenner, "Blood for the Ghosts," in *New Approaches to Ezra Pound* ed. Eva Hesse (Berkeley: University of California Press, 1969), p. 337.

16. *Instigations* (New York: Boni & Liveright, 1920), p. 342.

17. Apostolos N. Athanassakis, *The Homeric Hymns* (Baltimore: Johns Hopkins Press, 1976), p. xii.

18. See Peter Makin, *Provence and Pound* (Berkeley: University of California Press, 1978) and Stuart Y. McDougal, *Ezra Pound and the Troubadour Tradition* (Princeton: Princeton University Press, 1972).

19. *Guide to Kulchur*, p. 108.

20. Ibid., p. 107.

CHAPTER II: MALATESTA'S POST-BAG

1. See *The Analyst* V, VI, VII, XI, and XIII (newsletter of the Department of English, Northwestern University, 1953-?).

2. Michael F. Harper, "Truth and Calliope: Ezra Pound's Malatesta," *PMLA* 96 (1981): p. 99.

3. *Guide to Kulchur*, p. 1.

4. Ibid.

5. Ibid., p. 159.

CHAPTER III: THE PRINTING HOUSE OF HELL

1. See *The Marriage of Heaven and Hell*, ed. Clark Emery (Coral Gables: University of Miami Press, 1963), plate 14.

2. Ibid., plate 15.

3. Emery, Introduction, *The Marriage of Heaven and Hell*, p. 69.

4. Max Nänny, "Oral Dimensions in Ezra Pound," *Paideuma* 6 (1977): 14.

5. *Guide to Kulchur*, p. 184.

6. Nänny, "Oral Dimensions in Ezra Pound," p. 16.

7. Quoted in *The Wisdom of China and India*, ed. Lin Yutang (New York: Modern Library, 1942), p. 812.

8. Nänny, "Oral Dimensions in Ezra Pound," p. 20.

9. Eugene Eoyang, "The Confucian Odes," *Paideuma* 3 (1974): 33.

CHAPTER IV: CIVIC ACCOUNTS

1. John Ruskin, *The Stones of Venice*, (New York: Hurst), 2: 280.

2. Terisio Pignatti, *The Doges Palace* (New York: Reynal, 1965), p. 6.

3. See Carroll F. Terrell, "A Couple of Documents," *Paideuma* 6 (1977): 360-61.

4. See D.J. Hugen, "Small Birds of Cyprus," *Paideuma* 3 (1974): 230-38.

5. See John Peck, "Arras and Painted Arras," *Paideuma* 3 (1974): 60-66.

6. Hugh Kenner, *The Pound Era* (Berkeley: University of California Press, 1971), pp. 114-16.

7. See Wendy Flory, *Ezra Pound and "The Cantos"* (New Haven: Yale University Press, 1980), pp. 130-39.

8. See Sharon Mayer Libera, "Casting His Gods Back into the NOUS: Two Neoplatonists and *The Cantos* of Ezra Pound," *Paideuma* 2 (1973): 355-77.

9. *Guide to Kulchur*, p. 224.

CHAPTER V: PRESIDENTIAL CORRESPONDENCE

1. Stock, *The Life of Ezra Pound*, pp. 294-97.
2. *Jefferson and/or Mussolini* (London: Stanley Nott, 1935) p. 15.
3. See Robert M. Knight, "Thomas Jefferson in Canto XXXI," *Paideuma* 5 (1976): 79-93.
4. See William Chace, *The Political Identities of Ezra Pound and T.S. Eliot* (Stanford: Stanford University Press, 1973), pp. 50-55.
5. *Impact: Essays on Ignorance and the Decline of American Civilization*, p. 269.
6. See Stephen Fender, *The American Long Poem* (London: Edward Arnold, 1977), pp. 111-33.
7. *Impact: Essays on Ignorance and the Decline of American Civilization*, p. 179.
8. Galbraith, *Money: Whence It Came, Where It Went* (Boston: Houghton Mifflin, 1975), pp. 53-54.

CHAPTER VI: SIENESE BANK CHARTERS

1. See Ben Kimpel and T.C. Duncan Eaves, "The Sources of Cantos XLII and XLIII," *Paideuma* 6 (1977): 333-58; "The Sources of the Leopoldine Cantos," *Paideuma* 7 (1978): 249-77; and "Pound's Use of Sienese Manuscripts for Cantos XLII and XLIII," *Paideuma* 8 (1979): 513-18.
2. Kearns, *Guide to Ezra Pound's "Selected Cantos"* (New Brunswick: Rutgers University Press, 1980), p. 103.
3. See "The Periplus of Hanno," ed. Carroll F. Terrell, *Paideuma* 1 (1972): 223-28.
4. Kimpel and Eaves, "The Sources of Cantos XLII and XLIII," p. 338.
5. Giuseppe Gagliani, "Montis Pascuorum," *Yale Literary Magazine* 127 (1958): 18-23.
6. Galbraith, *Money: Whence It Came, Where It Went*, p. 18.

CHAPTER VII: CHINESE MIRRORS

1. See Robert Demott, "Ezra Pound and Charles Bowlker: Note on Canto LI," *Paideuma* 1 (1972): 189-98.
2. See Daniel Pearlman, *The Barb of Time* (New York: Oxford University Press, 1969), pp. 172-210, 304-11.
3. See William Tay, "Between Kung and Eleusis: *Li Chi*, The Eleusinian Rites, Erigena and Ezra Pound," *Paideuma* 4 (1975): 37-54.
4. See Carroll F. Terrell, "History, de Mailla, and the Dynastic Cantos," *Paideuma* 5 (1976): 95-121; David Gordon, "The Sources of Canto LIII," *Paideuma* 5 (1976): 123-52; John J. Nolde, "The Sources for Canto LIV: Part One," *Paideuma* 5 (1976): 419-53; idem, "The Sources for Canto LIV: Part Two," *Paideuma* 6 (1977): 45-98; idem, "The Sources for Canto LV," *Paideuma* 7 (1978): 189-247; idem, "The Sources for Chinese Dynastic Canto LVI," *Paideuma* 8 (1979): 263-92; idem, "The Sources for Chinese Dynastic Canto LVI: Part Two," *Paideuma* 8 (1979): 485-511.
5. Nolde, "The Sources for Canto LIV: Part One," p. 420.
6. David Gordon, "Confucius, Philosophe, An Introduction to the Chinese Cantos 52-61," *Paideuma* 5 (1976): 397-98.
7. Wendy Flory, *Ezra Pound and "The Cantos,"* p. 156.
8. Terrell, *A Companion to "The Cantos of Ezra Pound"* (Berkeley: University of California Press, 1980), 1: 214.

CHAPTER VIII: THE ADAMS PAPERS

1. See Frederick K. Sanders, *John Adams Speaking* (Orono: University of Maine Press, 1975).
2. Page Smith, *John Adams* (New York: Doubleday, 1962), 1: 79.
3. *The Works of John Adams*, ed. Charles Francis Adams (Boston: Little, Brown, 1856), 1: 130.
4. *The Works of John Adams*, 1: 138.
5. Smith, *John Adams*, 2: 701.

CHAPTER IX: THE PISAN BLACK-OUT

1. See Christine Brooke-Rose, *A ZBC of Ezra Pound* (London: Faber and Faber, 1971), p. 10.
2. See Leon Surette, *A Light from Eleusis* (Oxford: Clarendon Press, 1979), pp. 179-89.
3. See Walter B. Michaels, "Pound and Erigena," *Paideuma* 1 (1972): 37-54.
4. See Massimo Bacigalupo, *The Forméd Trace: The Later Poetry of Ezra Pound* (New York: Columbia University Press, 1980), pp. 142-49.
5. *Guide to Kulchur*, p. 152.
6. See Bryant Knox, "Allen Upward and Ezra Pound," *Paideuma* 3 (1974): 71-83, and A.D. Moody, "Pound's Allen Upward," *Paideuma* 4 (1975): 55-70.
7. See Thomas Grieve, "Annotations to the Chinese in *Section: Rock-Drill*," *Paideuma* 4 (1975): 362-508. I am indebted to Grieve's analyses of the ideograms throughout this section.
8. Lin Yutang, *The Wisdom of China and India*, pp. 696-97.
9. Ibid., p. 737.

CHAPTER X: A MEMORIAL TO ARCHIVISTS AND LIBRARIANS

1. For the various documents that Pound used in this section, see James J. Wilhelm, *The Later Cantos of Ezra Pound* (New York: Walker, 1977), pp. 64-147.
2. Thomas Hart Benton, *Thirty Years' View* (New York: D. Appleton, 1854), 1: iv.
3. Wilhelm, *The Later Cantos of Ezra Pound*, p. 74.
4. Benton, *Thirty Years' View*, 1: 236.
5. See James Neault, "Apollonius of Tyana," *Paideuma* 4 (1975): 4-36.
6. Wilhelm, *The Later Cantos of Ezra Pound*, p. 93.
7. See Wilhelm, *The Later Cantos of Ezra Pound*, pp. 102-19.
8. William Dudley Foulke, Introduction, *History of the Langobards* (New York: Longmans, Green, 1906), p. xlii.
9. Ibid.
10. See Carroll F. Terrell, "*The Eparch's Book* of Leo the Wise," *Paideuma* 2 (1973): 223-60, and Jules Nicole, "*The Eparch's Book*: Greek and Latin Redaction," *Paideuma* 2 (1973): 261-311.
11. Terrell, "*The Eparch's Book* of Leo the Wise," p. 227.
12. Ivan Ducjev, Introduction, *The Book of the Eparch* (London: Variorum Reprints, 1970), p. vii.
13. Ibid.
14. Wilhelm, *The Later Cantos of Ezra Pound*, pp. 121-22.

15. See David Gordon, "The Sacred Edict," *Paideuma* 3 (1974): 169-90.

16. See Wilhelm, *The Later Cantos of Ezra Pound*, pp. 138-47.

17. F.W. Baller, Preface, *The Sacred Edict* (Shanghai: American Presbyterian Mission Press, 1892), p. iv.

18. Ibid., p. iii.

19. Gordon, "The Sacred Edict," p. 174.

20. Ibid., p. 180.

21. Wilhelm, *The Later Cantos of Ezra Pound*, p. 143.

CHAPTER XI: FINAL DOCUMENTS: COKE AND ROCK

1. See David Gordon, "Edward Coke: The Azalia is Grown," *Paideuma* 4 (1975): 223-99.

2. J.C. Holt, *Magna Carta* (Cambridge: Cambridge University Press, 1965), p. 16.

3. Ibid., p. 18.

4. Ibid., p. 8.

5. See Carroll F. Terrell, "The Na-Khi Documents I: The Landscape of Paradise," *Paideuma* 3 (1974): 91-122, and John Peck, "Landscape as Ceremony in the Later Cantos: From 'The Roads of France' to 'Rock's World,'" *Agenda* 9 (1971): 26-69.

6. Joseph Rock, *The Ancient Na-Khi Kingdom of Southwest China* (Cambridge: Harvard University Press, 1947), 1: 270.

7. See Wilhelm, *The Later Cantos of Ezra Pound*, pp. 170-75.

Index